Survival
Time

Survival
Time

A HANDBOOK FOR SURVIVING A VIOLENT INCIDENT

Wayne R Hill PhD

Aimee E Olivas MA

ISBN: 1516868668
ISBN 13: 9781516868667

Table of Contents

Introduction

Violent incidents are steadily on the increase in this country, and we, the authors of this survival manual, have determined that most people are unaccustomed and ill-prepared to deal with violent situations. Hence, the purpose of this manual is to help you better understand the actions of violent people (perpetrators). Most importantly, the chief focus is on your actions to help you survive a violent incident. Our goal is to help you understand the strategies for protecting yourself until emergency services personnel (i.e. police, fire, and medical) arrive and gain control of the situation. Our primary message is that you, the reader, are the first line of defense as a crisis intervention specialist.

In the early years of our nation's history, authorities such as the Night Watchmen, while walking on rounds in the night, sang out, "It is midnight, and all is well"; they helped the citizens of a community feel safe. But it was the citizens of a community who were responsible for capturing and punishing criminals. However, for a lot of reasons, communities gave up vigilante justice, handing over their law-enforcement and justice duties to a government agent such as a sheriff, constable, or town marshal. The final move was to establish a municipal police department, and it was at that point that citizens gave over all law-enforcement responsibilities to the police.

As law-enforcement procedures evolved, the attitudes of communities changed. Now most people believe that police officers are trained to intervene in criminal cases and/or crisis management. This seems straightforward and simple on the face of it, but it is not. Police procedure, logistics, command responsibilities, local and state policies, and other factors complicate matters. Police intervention in violent incidents is also significantly complicated by the perpetrators. Perpetrators are complex human beings; their emotional, physical, and cognitive characteristics determine who they are and how they will act.

Obviously, many variables may influence or cause some people to act out violently, but it is impossible to determine why perpetrators initiate violent action. We cannot even be sure whether a person who has been violent in the past will act out again if placed in a particular situation. Even if we know certain discrete factors about a potential perpetrator such as personal values, family relationships, and the ability to resolve problems, identifying the right combination that would become a catalyst for violence is so complex that it is impossible to predict who will act out violently.

Taking the above hypothesis into account—that police intervention is not always possible, and we cannot isolate life factors that will identify perpetrators—we are going to concentrate our efforts to a new way of thinking. Our goal is to help you become survival-smart and improve your chances of surviving a violent incident.

You must also take into account a victim's commitment to stay alive, including his or her background, attitude, and the willingness to do what is necessary. At one time in my life, I, Dr. Hill, believed that everyone would fight to survive when the chips were down. However, after a tour of duty in Vietnam, coupled with years of policing, I came to recognize this belief is not true. Instead, I now believe that there are degrees of willingness to fight for survival. For instance, some people give up too soon in a crisis for various reasons. Others do not believe they have the right to survive at the cost of taking the life of another. Some are committed to staying alive but simply do not know how to engage in a life-saving process. Still others become so overwhelmed that confusion takes over. For instance, people may run in circles, starting and stopping, as they change their minds about whether to do this or that but end up doing nothing. Such behavior is one aspect of *cognitive dissonance*. That is when a person believes strongly in two concepts that are diametrically opposed to each other. Because oppositional beliefs create tension, the tension must be reduced and resolved. It is our purpose to clarify survival options by helping you understand how to act, despite the dissonance you may face as a victim.

We present this handbook to help you understand the initial response victims may have in a crisis situation and to arm you with specific actions to influence your behavior in the particular violent circumstances you may find yourself in. Ultimately, *you* are the first line of defense for surviving a violent incident.

CHAPTER 1

Innate Reactions to Violence

Confusion, fear, shock, denial, and crisis response are the most typical reactions to violence. As a violent incident unfolds, most witnesses, both observers on the periphery of violence and victims, experience confusion as an initial response because violent acts seem so out of place. Witnesses and victims get caught off-guard and become further confused in the violent circumstances. They most often do not know what is happening, nor do they have a clue about engaging in survival thinking and taking appropriate survival action.

In contrast, this would not have been the case for ancient humans, who, throughout the day, remained on guard for their natural enemies and predators. In today's society, people in an extremely unfamiliar situation will resort to behavior they are most familiar with or behavior that is most closely associated with past experiences. This suggests that most individuals who have never been in a violent incident would not likely engage in positive survival activity.

Drive Reduction/Tension Reduction

Ironically, in accordance with drive reduction/tension reduction theory, human beings are required, unconsciously, to take some action in a crisis situation. Therefore, they resort to preprogrammed behavior or some action, such as fight or flee. Humans are creatures who respond or take action that will meet needs to survive. At the most fundamental level, such needs are simple, straightforward, and easy to understand. For example, humans need to breathe air to survive. If the oxygen is in some way depleted or removed, tension builds rapidly while the victim desperately tries to meet the conditions of this need state. To test this theory, you only need to hold your breath to discover that tension begins to build and will continue to build until you are compelled to take a breath so that you take in life-giving oxygen. You will find that you cannot hold your breath until you die; you will breathe. This is in keeping with Maslow's Hierarchy of Needs. Primary needs such as water, shelter, and food take precedence over all other needs. Yet it is clear that we humans have secondary needs, such as the need for community, friendship, fellowship, and family. These other needs, while not basic, can make life more pleasant.

Secondary needs are more similar to wants than to needs—for example, the need for autonomy. Humans enjoy being in charge of their own lives, but when that opportunity is denied (at work, at home, in a social situation, etc.), they have a drive to change the situation so that they return to maintaining power over their own life choices.

When a person or organism is in a need state—whether primary or secondary—the person will become motivated to engage in action that is called a *drive*. Drive equates to energy expressed toward meeting a need. Drive will be strengthened concurrently with a need state because it builds in severity. This condition may be more clearly expressed as tension.

Tension builds up, forcing the organism—in this case, a person—to engage in tension-reduction actions. As tension reduction is accomplished, drive reduction is also accomplished, if only momentarily. One might say that increased tension causes an action to reduce that tension because increased tension places the person in a position of dealing with a range of discomfort, from mild to extremely unbearable.

In contrast, when tension discomfort is diminished, so is tension reduction, simultaneously. Because violence propels people into a need state due to the potential for loss of one's life, individuals feel both drive reduction and tension reduction. We believe that understanding tension reduction strategies in a violent crisis may increase survival opportunities.

Victim Behavior during a Violent Incident

Common victim behavior implies that in the midst of a violent attack, a person will have few options available from which to make a good choice. Furthermore, without preparation, almost all of the choices one may make will likely be faulty. As violence ensues, a victim's state of being will normally transition into "blind panic," or the inability to logically think during a crisis. That is the hallmark of traditional victim behavior.

Sometimes, at the first indication of totally unexpected violence, some victims think that someone is playing a practical joke on everyone, as was the case in the mass shooting at the movie theatre in Aurora, Colorado. This feeling of denial can even affect those people who may be a bit more aware and informed than others, such as those who have gained theoretical knowledge from having read articles or books, attended seminars, and/or watched television specials about violence or violent perpetrators. And while such people are theoretically knowledgeable about violence, they are still no better off than others due to a lack of life experience, or at least experiential or "hands-on" training. So they, and others, retreat into denial and do nothing, which, unless part of an overall strategy, is likely the worst thing to do.

Because most people are unfamiliar with crisis brought on by severe violence, it is worth noting that the "freeze" instinct is the default response out of the three most basic choices: fight, flee, or freeze. Freezing most likely originates from primitive humans in a dangerous hunting situation in which they became the prey. Because the human brain is designed to respond to motion, a predator often relies on a victim's movement as the cue to strike. This creates a paradox. In the lower animal world, no matter where an animal is on the food chain, it has a natural enemy or predator. Typically mothers of prey teach their young to be perfectly still until the threat has passed. Interestingly, for human beings, the freeze response has evolved into modern-day parental control words during early child development. The extension or the translation of the freeze response has evolved into the parental command to "stop," combined with the correct vocal cue when a child is in imminent danger. The command "Stop!" in combination with a certain intonation translates to the child to go no farther or the result will be disastrous.

For example, a child about to run into the street who simultaneously sees and hears a control figure, such as a parent, will learn to freeze in place in a corresponding response to the command "stop." Humans have an evolutionary capacity to learn, rather quickly, the correct response to the command words "stop" and "no," as well as other command words indicating danger. Furthermore, due to paired associative learning, in this case, the tone of the voice used by the parent paired with the word "stop" causes a visceral response that shocks a child into stopping.

As a child grows older, and in the absence of violent experiences, victims of indiscriminate violence generalize. In doing so, they choose to freeze as the response of choice. Ironically, it is at that very moment that one of our most important, adaptive, life-saving evolutionary traits will likely result in death during an indiscriminate mass-murder incident. One might say the freeze response has allowed humans to endure and evolve over the ages, but this trait then becomes the obstacle to survival during a life-threatening crisis such as mass murder. A person may deduce that if there is a chance of not being attacked as long as he is undetectable, makes no aggressive movement, or does not, in some manner, telegraph resistance, he may survive a natural predator. Keep in mind that just because a person cannot see a predator does not mean one is not nearby.

Humans could not have learned to live together and rely on one another if it were not for the inherent capacity to adapt to the civilization/socialization process. Through evolution, humans first created a system in which they followed a very simple set of rules. Over the ages, those simple rules have evolved into a complex set of rules that have transitioned into laws, along with the criminal justice system. In so doing, humans have handed over their community responsibilities to the criminal justice system, which is composed of the police, courts, and adjunct agencies. Now, because members of a civilized society are well conditioned to obey commands, it takes concentrated effort to become a free thinker during a severe, life-threatening crisis. This is especially true when considering the influence of two concepts, the *deindividuation effect* and the *herding effect*. The deindividuation effect means stop thinking and let the rising panic, anger, or frustration cause a person to join in violent or other criminal acts. In the herding effect, people often lose their nerve and run like hell with the herd, even if the herd is running over the cliff's edge.

Fight, Flee, or Freeze

The question remains: What does a person do about a violent incident when there appears to be no tension-reduction solutions within his or her experiential repertoire? In other words, what does a person do when no action he or she is familiar with reduces the tension and co-occurring anxiety and panic? The answer is that people often choose one of three primary default actions: fight, flee, or freeze.

Violence may bring on instant disorientation, which again often leads victims to do nothing constructive. The consequence of this is a sudden realization that the crisis is real, and panic strikes. Denial is replaced by fight, flee, or freeze behavior. Violence most often catches victims so totally unaware that a significant number of people react like a deer caught in headlights or a rabbit caught in a spotlight. Freezing is a natural response, and there is certainly a time and place for the freeze response; however, the wrong time is when a perpetrator is actively trying to kill people and you could become a casualty of collateral damage.

We discuss these three choices further in following chapters. For now, however, at the very least, these three default choices allow the victim to obey the rule of survival on some unconscious level. The freeze or flee reactions are low-level responses to survival complexities and often will not fulfill survival requirements. In one scenario, a person hopes not to be seen but is about to jump out of her own skin while the anxiety (tension) builds up. During this time, the victim's enemies have her right in the crosshairs. The other situation involves victims fleeing for their lives, running full out without a plan, unaware of what is going on around them, completely fear-driven. Both scenarios place these people at risk and illustrate the need for potential victims to know and apply appropriate survival actions.

Traditional Thinking

Historically, Americans have lived in a country in which, except for random stranger-to-stranger crime like robbery or theft, most Americans have enjoyed living the "feel safe fantasy." We call it a fantasy because violent incidents are occurring all around us every day. Because we are insulated from the knowledge of them, they are not part of our conscious reality except for a momentary reminder during the evening news. Americans believe the only real adjustment they need to take with regard to mainstream violence is to avoid identified danger zones (i.e., violence in certain geographical areas). In the process, it appears that with each new generation, we have become more like sheep, following one after another, oblivious to danger, living the fantasy.

Further complicating matters, people now maintain more effective mobility. We can get into a car, which acts as a secure cubicle, and drive away. In contrast, those who came before us did not have it so easy. They knew that survival depended on consistently making the effort to remain aware of changes in their environment. Ironically, human success, as a civilized society, has been its downfall. Throughout the evolution of our society, we have mistakenly come to believe that protecting ourselves is synonymous with taking the law into our own hands, which is absurd. However, being responsible and taking active responsibility for our own safety is one of the cornerstones upon which this nation was built. And contrary to our belief that we can just drive away from violence, we now have violent people bringing the problem to our front doors.

Most Americans have enjoyed an extended period of uncommon and relative peace. For the most part, even during isolated periods of unrest, our citizens have come to expect that their safety is somehow guaranteed. This fantasy is reflected in the people who want to know how a mass murder could occur and why police didn't stop the crime. It is exactly this type of naïveté that puts people at greatest risk. Even the police are targeted as victims, lulled into believing that because of their position, and because they carry firearms, they are safer than other people. Because police officers are often America's scapegoats, very little will be learned from the investigation of a violent incident in the way of self-protection because, once again, the focus will be on profiling (i.e., who committed this terrible act rather than how people can act to save themselves from disaster). This handbook is devoted to educating you about self-survival.

Failure of Traditional Actions

The 2007 Virginia Polytechnic University (Virginia Tech) massacre is one more in a series of tragic events that highlight the importance of a departure from an old way of thinking to embrace the new. Traditionally, in the aftermath of catastrophic, violent events, we, as a nation, have focused on the perpetrators, developing criminal profiles, looking for responsible parties, and pointing the blame finger, as we Monday-morning-quarterback the police, FBI, or whoever may be in the media "crosshairs." The traditional philosophy is that we can stop violence if we can isolate who is to blame and identify their motives. That's an important tenet, without doubt, but it addresses just one side of a two-sided equation. Just assigning blame provides a false sense of security, as if to say, "Because we now know who did it and why they did it, it is less likely to happen again."

On the face of it, based on the way in which our society has functioned historically, it all seems to make sense. The indignant rhetoric can be heard— "Let's put a stop to these people"—as if all mass murderers have taken the same seminar on the best way to kill a lot of people. It is a comforting thought and a worthy fantasy as we hear a resounding, collective "Amen!" That kind of information can cause people to feel informed. Naturally, the more understanding a person has about criminal acts, the better off he or she will be. But as anyone can see, profiling has not stopped mass murderers, terrorists, serial killers, mad bombers, or other sinister criminal acts or activists. In the aftermath of one of these tragedies, law enforcement can say, "He fits the profile." Unfortunately, the puzzle is solved after the violent incident occurs and victim is dead.

Seldom do we remember that a lot of people in our society are hanging on by a thread. Rich or poor, educated or not, smart or less smart, articulate or not, many people are just barely managing, dying to be heard and willing to harm and/or kill those who will not listen. These murderers believe in punishing those who will not listen to them. However, much of the time, we do not listen because what these people have to say is just illogical, and if we tried to listen, they would dominate our lives with crazed, meaningless babbling. These people will present themselves at the workplace, in public spaces, and in colleges and schools, and they have very diverse backgrounds.

For example, one day, "weird" Bill shows up at the office with a gun and starts killing people. Of course Bill's family is stunned by this and does not know what happened to him. Fundamentally, in the moment of crisis, it doesn't matter what triggered Bill's behavior; all that matters is that the victims get out of Bill's way and get out of the incident alive.

The Virginia Tech incident is just the kind of event that causes people with severe mental illness, who were just hanging on, to let go. It is not smart to get comfortable with the idea that "It was so awful that it's not likely to happen again." A more logical response is to gain awareness of the tools everyone possesses to have a better possibility of surviving a crisis situation. That is the purpose of this book.

Law Enforcement and Management of Violent Incidents

People are invested in the criminal justice system and have trained themselves to "let them handle it." It is this evolution, from ancient times to the modern era that has been necessary for our ability to live together and to establish family and communal life. Communal living comes at a price, though. Through the process of socialization, people have dispensed with their more primitive reactions to violence. For example, the age-old handshake has turned into a common greeting rather than a demonstration of an open, extended hand, meaning no intended harm. Even in more ancient times, shaking hands did not mean that a person trusted another before getting to know each other. This is sound advice for protecting yourself. You can be friendly, but you must stay on guard. Observe the whole person while maintaining a friendly demeanor, if that seems appropriate. Remember, there are a lot of ways you can be hurt that do not involve physical danger from another person.

Be reminded that you should be careful who you become friends with. There are a lot of recorded rapes on campuses in which a person becomes the victim of such a crime by letting someone get too close by being too trusting. On a conscious level, humans appear to have lost the ability to read subtle cues transmitted from others that telegraph an intention to engage in harmful behavior. In addition, people appear to have lost the conscious ability to pick up on olfactory sensations that transmit fear, danger, or the intent to harm. Regaining an awareness of ancient and primitive survival skills is necessary to prevent people from depending solely on law-enforcement authorities to protect them. It would be wishful thinking to believe that law enforcement will always be in the right place to protect the community.

To those who would say, "Give us more police, and we will be more secure," we must consider the irrationality of such beliefs. It would be impossible, in a free society, to field enough police officers to prevent violent incidents. How could a school or university ever post a police officer or security officer in every building? I remember the advent of high-tech policing. One major change that took place was the elimination of a daily "hot sheet," a list of stolen cars reported in the previous twenty-four-hour period. It was replaced with reams of computer printouts, multiple times a week, for each street cop. The officers had asked for data, and the new computer wizards generated so much information, which included all crime reports compiled in a twenty-four-hour period, that officers were unable to process all the data before the next printout landed in their laps. Ironically, there was so much information that officers were unable to use it.

We wish the police could always be there for every person, guarding and protecting. But it is not true; they will not be and cannot be because they are physically unable to, and it is folly to believe that law-enforcement authorities will always be able to save everyone and set things right. As a former Dallas police officer, I spent my career dealing with the fallout in the aftermath of one crisis episode after another, recognizing that it was an ongoing effort to protect community members.

As with most police officers, I was well trained in the crime-prevention strategy of trying to appear omnipresent. The training also included assisting victims after the fact, recording information, processing crime scenes, questioning witnesses, and, on rare occasions, concurrently arresting criminal perpetrators. It is important to know that law enforcement rarely catches hard-core criminals in the act of committing a crime. Police investigators track down and arrest criminals, but street officers are principally clean-up specialists who make arrests *after* a crime has been committed. Officers are often categorized as first responders. First responders may provide useful information to secondary specialists, such as detectives or investigators, that may lead to an arrest. As hard as police agencies and police officers try, they are almost never in a position to prevent an event like a mass murder. That is why we are absolutely dedicated to the belief that you can become your own best survival resource by being self-trained in awareness.

In the absence of planned assistance during violent situations, a person must act independently and in that way become autonomous. Autonomous action means to advocate for your own safety. Most people do not give much thought to their autonomy; most people do not realize that they await a cue or social command before responding to a situation. The most powerful of such commands are "no," "don't," "stop," "go," and other more sophisticated commands. Still, patterns of our lives or the way we live our lives lead most people to believe falsely that they are autonomous (i.e., acting independently for the sake of their own lives).

In truth, people go unwittingly down life's road making many mundane decisions, oblivious to the fact that society is set up to inhibit autonomy. Most people have little autonomy under the guise of exercising free will, and society works well that way. Frankly, a strong society probably *should* function that way. Lives would probably run smoothly, if only people would stop breaking the rules, many of which have been converted into those pesky laws we discussed earlier. These laws are in place as a proactive, preventative measure so there will be no doubt whether acts or omissions are permitted or explicitly forbidden. Keep in mind that the rules and laws are in place because someone has already violated a custom or a norm, and a law has to be enacted to compensate for and try to prevent future misdeeds.

Identifying Suspects

There are well-defined laws against murder, which is one of our strongest cultural taboos because it is a heinous act. Oddly enough, however, murder is one of the crimes that is hard to prevent. As a society, humans tend to tolerate a little theft or burglary, but we do everything possible to discourage murder. Yet there is a population of people, from all walks of life, all the way up the crime index, who will murder others. It is interesting to note that those who will commit murder often do not recognize that potential within themselves. However, there is another segment of people who have engaged in or will engage in murder, knowing this action will occur before they do it, because some of these murderers have envisioned their murderous thoughts for years, until they finally act them out. Eventually, this group becomes overwhelmed with the impulse to kill, which rises to the surface. People will say they never saw it coming, and most will want to know what the "trigger" was. The trigger doesn't matter because some individuals simply plan to engage in murderous behavior.

Perhaps most of us have known someone at work or school who fits several points of a profile regarding a mass murderer, as established by the FBI. It is important to note that people who seem to fit the profile may never commit a crime. Consider this dilemma: even if a person appears to fit the profile of a potential murderer, it would be practically impossible for the police to provide a stakeout, day after day, month after month. It would also be illegal to arrest someone who has a psychiatric history or fits the profile before he or she has committed a crime. So trying to report a suspicious person without evidence to authorities may cause a person to appear paranoid or a harbinger of disaster. The authorities may believe that a person reporting suspicious behavior is unstable if she talks to them frequently about a suspect and may find herself the target of an investigation.

Therefore, for the authorities to take a concern seriously, a person would need to provide them with a report that includes concrete information, such as proof of a plan by someone who intends to hurt others. This seems unlikely to happen, except in the aftermath of a violent incident, when people will come forward and say, "I knew he was acting strangely because he said or did X, Y, or Z." The best choice would be to quietly keep an eye on the person of interest so that you will be less likely to be taken by surprise and avoid becoming a victim.

Conclusion

When there are no police officers to help, it will be up to you to save yourself, so the question becomes "How *do* I help myself?" Chances are that you are not prepared to survive a shooting situation. Most people do not know what to do when they find themselves in the middle of a violent event, especially a catastrophic violent event like the Virginia Tech mass murders. We hope to provide a very practical education, one that does not require you to become a boxer, martial arts practitioner, or firearms expert. In fact, we would prefer that you not focus on such things until you have a chance to master the simple concepts in this survival guide. By learning these simple concepts, you will not need to become a certified warrior or athlete. But you do need to be smart about your limitations and shore up any weaknesses. The primary objective is to stay alive and unharmed, if possible, until rescued.

Once you learn to see and assess your surroundings with survival in mind, you can begin to protect yourself. This book will teach a new way of thinking that embraces the idea of taking responsibility for your own survival. No one can do it for you; you must cross that bridge alone. Getting across that bridge requires serious consideration, dedication and commitment. Surviving a violent crisis or being a willing, compliant victim is often a choice. You need to commit to a new way of thinking, one that embraces the fundamental concept that you are the key to your survival. By gaining insight and understanding, you will recognize that your life is sacred and your responsibility to protect.

CHAPTER 2

Unmasking Violence

By
Aimee Olivas, MA, Forensic Psychology

Although some people may believe they know what a murderer looks like, they are wrong. Some individuals have images of a large lumbering figure, seething with hate, beset by madness, or perhaps disfigured in some way. Is that the picture that emerges in your mind? If so, this image is incorrect. The picture of a monstrous being has been perpetuated by a belief that only a monster could commit monstrous crimes. It is a myth that a violent offender is someone easily detected, someone who noticeably stands out from the rest of society, someone grotesque.

On the contrary, killers and other violent offenders typically go unnoticed, resembling an unremarkable, average person. Some actually seek to blend in with the rest of society or quietly withdraw for one reason or another, fading into the background like a piece of furniture that no one notices. Some live a life of seclusion, writing complicated and/or rambling declarations or manifestos, filled with paranoid ideation (psychosis), letting the pot simmer while planning to finally act out. And so new questions emerge: What do we know about murderers? Are they really different from each other, at their core?

To understand more about the crime of murder, in the beginning it is important to differentiate among types of murder and, secondly, what the murderer is trying to accomplish (i.e., the motive.) In this way, you will get a sense of what to expect should you get caught in the middle of a violent incident.

Overview

Violence can strike at any time and any place. One of the most tragic was the Columbine High School massacre that occurred on April 20, 1999. It was difficult to comprehend the violent acts of the two Columbine adolescents, who had planned and carried out their plan to murder as many people as possible at their school. At that time, in 1999, the Columbine assaults and murders were the first in a series of violent and severe crimes committed within an educational institution. Residents in the community were deeply alarmed when word of the attack circulated and they immediately contacted law-enforcement agencies. Authorities responded and were on the scene within minutes. However, having little or no intervention training with incidents of mass murder in schools, the police set up the scene in keeping with familiar tactics, using a traditional hostage-negotiations approach.

At the conclusion of the crisis, police agencies and their officers were criticized by local residents, as well as thousands of other people across the nation. People felt that police and school personnel should have been prepared for such an incident. Response time became an issue. Critics made comments such as "too little too late" and "The police did not protect our children." Then bandwagon drum bangers began thundering away. They targeted the lack of foreseeability, among other issues, implying that ill-fitting tactics and the lack of experience were no excuse for not anticipating such incidents. The public asked, "How could the authorities not be prepared for a Columbine-type event?" Other castigative remarks followed.

Critics did not take into consideration that the police were not trained to manage a mass-murder crime, in progress, in particular within an educational setting such as a public school, college, or university. Instead, critics argued that the lack of foresight and poor preparedness were scandalous, not to mention irresponsible. This is clear evidence of how little the general public understands the limitations of police training and enforcement. Looking back now, neither the public nor the police were aware that the nation was witnessing a new and growing trend of violence; it was as if Americans were blind while this new trend unfolded.

As the future became the present, authorities would improve their efforts in response to this new kind of violence; response time and on-scene effectiveness steadily advanced. Schools and universities would develop safety plans, some of which were part window dressing, part practical, but students would feel safer. In actuality, they would not be safer.

Still, with all the catch-up improvements toward more effective security, there remained, then and now, an unsettling and central issue that is couched in two parts that organizations cannot effectively address. The first part is, "What does a victim do when caught in a situation that leaves him or her without an organizationally designed safety net?" The second part is, "When you find yourself stuck in the middle of violence, what do you do when the shooting starts?" As stated, violence can occur at any time and any place; in fact, it is occurring some place right now.

There may be resistance to a philosophy of self-reliance that includes self-protection. Some may argue about time expenditure weighed against return on investment. Others may be quick to say that mass murder does not happen often enough to warrant an alteration in our thinking, leading to a change in our habits. Or they may say that there are overwhelming odds against a person being caught in such a tragedy. Our response is that, even if that is true, are you willing to take that gamble and stake your life on it? Consider how little effort it would take (comparatively speaking) to be better prepared.

The truth is, violence is occurring right now. What guarantee do you have that your home or the shopping center where you shop will not be the next place where violence strikes? When a severely violent incident occurs, such as mass murder, it takes on a life of its own. And, like a runaway freight train barreling downhill, whoever is caught on the track is in his or her private hell. There will be wreckage all around, and one may be just another piece in the pile. It will then be far too late to say, "I should have been prepared." Unfortunately, unprepared is exactly how the students and faculty of Columbine High School found themselves.

Unprepared

Unprepared is the way many people around the country felt in the spring of 1999. Unprepared is the way I felt as I embarked on a teaching career in Northern Virginia, months after the Columbine massacre.

I was hired as a high school teacher in Loudoun County, Virginia, in the fall of 1999. Although some time had passed since the Columbine incident, it remained an unpleasant memory, a sad moment in history, and one not likely to happen again, I hoped. Then, one week into the 2001 school year came the deadly 9/11 attacks, giving America and the rest of the world a new vision of violence. I was horrified by fiery, explosive images full of "real-time" death and destruction as I watched a second passenger jetliner crash into another of New York's twin towers. When I learned that another plane had crashed into the Pentagon, a structure only forty-five minutes away from the high school where I taught, and a place where some students' parents went to work each day, I felt hopeless.

The following year, the Beltway Sniper (or the DC Sniper) began randomly shooting victims in and around the Washington, DC, metro area. The victims included not only adults but also schoolchildren; no one was immune. Teachers were assigned to escort students to and from buses, just in case the DC Sniper exacted more violence near a school. Unfortunately, this safety procedure was just window dressing.

Nearly a decade later, the Virginia Tech shootings occurred. The Virginia Tech incident was very disturbing and heart wrenching to everyone. In the days following the Virginia Tech violence, my high school students wanted answers, and I felt an obligation to help them try to understand what had occurred. At the time, I was the resident psychology teacher, but I was at a loss for an explanation. They asked what kind of person does such a thing. Again at a loss, I felt confusion mixed with irony and totally out of my element. True, I taught the advanced psychology classes, but explaining the causes for violent behavior to adolescents proved difficult. I was not at all prepared to provide credible answers about mass murder. All of my lecture materials were in the abstract. My world of educating was turned on its ear; my knowledge was hypothetical. The students in our high school were in need of life-stabilizing answers, but there was much I could not reconcile. For example, Virginia Tech, as it is affectionately referred to by future students and alumni alike, is located in a small, rural town of Blacksburg, Virginia. How could this have happened in such a remote location? Isn't this kind violence more likely to happen in a large city?

Finding that I did not have adequate answers, I realized that I had a responsibility to students and others to help understand such issues. I felt a powerful obligation to understand why this kind of violence happens and what can be done to avert or minimize the risk of destruction, the likes of which had occurred at Virginia Tech. I now know that I needed those questions answered for my own sense of well-being, so I began the search for answers. The more in-depth I looked, the more consistently I found how little was known about preventing similar tragedies. I then began to seek answers by enrolling in Marymount University to acquire a master's degree in forensic psychology.

During that time, my father, a clinical psychologist who specialized in forensics and worked as a consultant and trainer to law-enforcement agencies, had begun thinking about similar questions. We began having teleconferences in 2007. Our discussions inevitably led us to one definite conclusion: in Virginia Tech-like events, the only person one can count on is oneself. There are, however, many other kinds of crisis situations in which others can provide pragmatic assistance. But with regard to campus mass murder, it is up to each individual to survive until law enforcement arrives. Therefore, being educated in survival techniques is the best way to accomplish that objective. People must be willing to devote a little time practicing how to think differently and to follow simple guidelines.

In the days following the Virginia Tech tragedy, my students were stunned. Even though I could provide little comfort, I told them the truth, which is that no one is ever safe from those who would do violence. The notion that some places exist within the confines of the United States where "this sort of thing does not happen" is mythical, and more importantly, is the type of myth that delivers unnecessary casualties.

I began introducing relevant factors for my students to think over because I believe that what you don't know will hurt you. It was surprising how little they knew about the potential for human destructiveness, cruelty, and savagery.

Most of their thoughts about violence focused on stranger-to-stranger acts, one person against another, or gang-related violence, which was the type of violence they were most familiar with. Conversely, I found that most of my students were not aware, until the Virginia Tech massacre, that a person must be prepared to survive. Being prepared requires more than simple acknowledgement that mass murderers exist; it requires knowing specific survival strategies.

Preparing for Violence

To be prepared, either systemically or individually, to survive a violent incident requires planning, enacting more specific laws, and educating the public. Most people who were aware of the mass killing of Virginia Tech students were troubled and confused. The student body grieved along with victims' friends and loved ones. There seemed to be a growing feeling of learned helplessness among the students, as if they had accepted that safety was no longer something that could be cultivated. After all, the incidents of mass shootings seemed random and unpredictable; anyone could be a mass murderer. That results in the feeling of an external locus of control or simply a force greater than oneself dictating one's fate. For example, one of my best friends at the time, a former teacher and now a full-time high school guidance counselor, confided that she, too, experienced confusion about how to respond in a potentially violent situation.

In the summer of 2007, a friend who was working on a graduate degree in guidance counseling arrived at my apartment door one afternoon to tell me a personal story that had left her feeling dismayed and full of self-doubt, especially in the wake of the Virginia Tech tragedy. She described a situation in which her "gut feeling" was to immediately leave a potentially explosive situation, yet she could not get up and take action, such as getting security involved.

As she and her peers met for their fifth evening class in multicultural counseling, she remembered her classmates entering the room and taking their usual seats, chatting with one another, and waiting for the professor to arrive. Instead, an unknown man appeared in the doorway of the classroom. The first thing she noticed about him was that he looked lost and out of place—so much so that one of her peers offered to help the man by asking him if he was looking for a specific class. The man responded that he was not looking for a specific class and asked which class the students were gathered for that evening. Again, a peer volunteered information to the man. Rather than leave the room and move on, the man entered the room and took a seat in the front of the class, folded his arms on the table, and leaned forward in a manner that my friend perceived as defensive. Furthermore, the mysterious man looked at each student individually and said nothing.

My friend told me that she felt a strange, hollow sensation in her stomach and began to experience feelings of panic. She turned to a classmate seated next to her and expressed her discomfort. Her classmate confided that she, too, felt the same way, yet neither one took the initiative to leave the room. After enduring approximately five minutes of threatening glances from this stranger, the professor arrived.

This is an example of cognitive dissonance. In this case, even with a prior violent event recently in the background, no one took any action to be preventive. Instead, due to dissonance, no one wanted to appear over reactive, and each concluded that nothing should be done because no one else was doing anything. So, ultimately, no one did anything. This process is circular; nothing is done because nothing is done. The civilization social apparatus suggests a message that "other people think mostly like me." While this message appears on the surface to be true, ironically, nothing could be further from the truth. Just because others around us dress similarly and seem to observe the same rules of society, it does not mean that there are not vast emotional differences among people. So we might justifiably ask, "How do we compensate if we cannot rely on first impressions or don't play 'follow the leader'?" We must start paying attention—not just while at the mall or at some other large gathering of people, but paying attention must become conscious and second nature. You can achieve this by teaching yourself to become aware until you are aware most, if not all, of the time. After all, it is not as if you would be doing something different from what you already do. You pay attention to things that are relevant and of interest to you. We suggest, therefore, that you must just expand your conscious awareness to include the mundane.

Introduction to Types of Murderers

Motive means everything with regard to categorization of murderers. It is within categorical understanding that a person begins to learn and, therefore, know more details about perpetrators. Without question, law-enforcement specialists dealing with the crime of murder have the experience and knowledge required to solve these cases. They are the experts and are absolutely needed. However, potential victims of a mass murderer can improve their chances of surviving such a crisis.

Perhaps, more often than not, the general public can gain much insight about murderers through an examination of an event, as well as from listening to interviews and personality testing done by professionals. Therefore, we will attempt to help you, the reader, know more about how murderers function.

Looking for a murderer is like looking for a needle in the proverbial haystack; murderers hide among us, appearing "normal" at first blush. There is no need to search for a monster; a murderer could potentially be anyone. Frankly, if they were easily identified, the police would have them locked up far in advance of their misdeeds, or at least before they could do much damage.

Why do some people commit murder when others do not? The answer is that the development of a murderer results from extreme factors (personality and/or developmental conditions) of one kind or another. For example, does a homicidal sociopath choose to kill due to extreme privilege so as to develop a sense of entitlement that is so out of balance because proper restraints (i.e., empathy and compassion) were not woven into the fabric of his personality? Or, conversely, is his drive toward murder due to having been treated extremely harshly, causing the continuous fear of death? In either case, what is the incentive to choose murder as an optional behavior? Clearly, these two factors are opposites, but their common thread is an unbalanced personality. One feature that aids in the propagation of a developing murderer is "damned if you do or damned if you don't." Another is that the murderer has no sense of caring for others who have simply become objects to do with as he or she so desires.

Having a basic understanding of the dynamics of a murderer's personality may help you formulate your plan of survival actions at a time when you will need to know your enemy better. Just because you do not have ill feelings toward someone (for whatever reason), do not be confused—at the time of the violent event, perpetrators are your enemies. This is true even, if prior to the violence, he or she was a friend or a friendly acquaintance. It is important not to rely on a prior positive relationship to save you.

Now let's consider the differences among categorical types of murders and then the similarities and differences among perpetrators of murder.

Murder as a Crime of Passion

Violence of this kind is born out of a heated dispute, fear of rejection, or impending rejection. The perpetrator may not have planned to carry out a murder; however, it may be during the course of an aggressive verbal exchange, the obsessive thoughts about the end of a relationship, or the anger that ensued as the victim turned his or her back on the offender that led to the murder. In each circumstance, anger was the motivation for murder. The case of Elisabeth "Betty" Broderick comes to mind when thinking about crimes of passion. Betty and her husband, Dan Broderick, were married for sixteen years. During the 1980s, Dan and Betty began to climb the social ladder. Dan developed a reputation as a successful California attorney, while Betty enjoyed her new status as a socialite. However, after sixteen years of marriage and three children, Dan left Betty for his much younger legal assistant, Linda Kolkena. Naturally, Betty was angry, humiliated, and discouraged, but rather than accept the rejection, Betty became obsessed with stopping the divorce in an attempt to keep Dan and prevent him from being with his new love interest, Linda. In fact, Betty spent approximately four years obsessing over Dan Broderick, his new life, and finally in 1989, his new wife. Unable to cope with the rejection, which was finalized by the new marriage, Betty killed Dan and his new wife in 1989; she fatally shot both of them as they lay sleeping in bed.

Stranger-to-Stranger Murder

The category of murder identified here is, for all intents and purposes, just as it sounds: one stranger to another. In this case, the offender and victim do not know one another, and often the victim is simply in the wrong place at the wrong time or stands as an obstacle in the way of the offender's goal. The victim is the cashier minding the convenience store, the pedestrian walking down a poorly lit street, or the homeowner who expected a quiet evening at home but forgot to lock the door. In each of these examples, the offender is motivated by greed to take what is not his. The cashier is killed for money, the pedestrian is mugged and killed for money and valuables, and the homeowner is killed while at home in a botched burglary attempt.

Serial Murder

Generally speaking, this kind of murder is one in a series of murders, perpetrated by the same person. Its frequency may be determined by seemingly unrelated events. A fresh murder may occur when internalized tension builds up inside the perpetrator, in which case the onset of the murder is dictated by the perpetrator's dynamic psychology, in such a manner that he or she feels driven to kill. Serial killers experience related physiological tension that may be elevated by a fantasy in which the perpetrator orchestrates and controls the outcome of the murder to meet the requirements of his or her fantasy.

Most professionals agree that during the murder, the perpetrator is a player in the fantasy. In this way, the perpetrator can more thoroughly enjoy the fantasy. It becomes more intimate. Such action would be the difference in watching a pornographic movie vs. actually playing a part in the movie. Of course, there are many other dynamics that are too numerous to address.

Popular culture has glamorized the serial murderer through various media sources. Fascination with serial killers has led many in society to view the serial killer as unique. Many people can easily recall names such as Ted Bundy, Richard Ramirez, and Jeffrey Dahmer. These same people would be hard pressed to identify the victims of serial killers. The serial murderer is an individual who is far more pathetic than unique because this individual does not empathize with others. In addition, these sociopathic killers feel no anxiety, not even when they engage in murderous behavior. At the same time, they seek to blend in with society and appear to follow its norms, while secretly selecting the next victim.

Serial murderers are predators. They hunt on the periphery of society, choosing vulnerable victims who happen to be in their hunting ground. Their victims are often persons whose absence will go unnoticed for days, weeks, or even months, and sometimes forever. For this population of killers, murder is a means to an end. It is a way to feel gratification. It is said that serial killers will often spend time with their victims, inflicting horrific, sadistic torturous acts on the victim's body, alive or dead. For example, serial killers often derive pleasure through masturbatory activity while watching their victims suffer.

Serial killers do not value human life; rather, they believe that other humans are to be used at their leisure. It is important to point out that not all antisocial people are serial murderers, but all serial killers are antisocial, narcissistic, and sociopathic. In this sense, other people serve the killer's needs. Serial killers violate the prohibition of law and culture without hesitation. They pay no attention to the rules of society.

A perfect and well-known example is the notorious serial killer, Jeffrey Dahmer. Dahmer appeared "normal" and well-adjusted on the surface, while beneath the surface was a lust-driven, seething, monstrous animal who acted out horrific cannibalistic fantasies. Classmates remember him as being shy, but having a sense of humor. Little did his classmates know about his rage, lust, perversions, and desire to kill. Dahmer was not recognized as a discipline problem in school, nor do people recall thinking of him as someone who presented an inherent danger to society. On the outside, Dahmer appeared to conform to societal norms, but when no one was looking and he could focus on himself, he engaged in private, ritualistic fantasies. When he began his journey toward murder, young Jeffrey Dahmer focused on killing and dismembering small creatures such as squirrels and cats. Eventually, as his fascination and arousal with violence grew, Dahmer's focus shifted to larger animals such as dogs, and finally to humans.

Dahmer's first murder was acted out as part of a long-running adolescent fantasy to kill a human being. His childhood impulses were enhanced by adult experiences. His *modus operandi* (MO) was to lure young men into his apartment, offer them a beverage laced with a sedative, and then kill them. He engaged in necrophilia, sexual intercourse with a corpse, and finally cannibalism.

Yet to look at Jeffrey Dahmer as he sat in court, one would not see a monstrous figure but a rather demure, distant, and emotionally unresponsive individual. Dahmer's quiet manner and passivity offered the impression of someone who was trustworthy and not capable of committing the heinous crimes he went to prison for.

Mass Murder

A mass murderer is an individual who typically catches the public by surprise. Typically, the mass murderer is someone who does not socialize well with others and feels intimidated by people. Often this individual struggles with making friends or getting along with others. The pervasive belief among this type of murderer is that he or she is misunderstood, and rather than attempt to reach outward to befriend someone, the killer recoils and focuses on him- or herself, work, or perhaps the development of a plan to commit a mass murder.

Individuals who have witnessed mass murders and learned the identity of the perpetrator typically recall that the person was quiet, withdrawn, reclusive, shy, and a little "odd." However, it is important to note that the overriding feature is not necessarily being withdrawn or shy, but rather the willingness to act out extreme violence.

Like the serial murderer and the spree murderer, the mass murderer often manifests symptoms of a personality disorder: narcissistic, antisocial, or dependent. Often this type of person is quietly enraged. He or she may be an *injustice detector*, perceiving that wrongs have been perpetrated against him or her, either by a singular person or by a group of people. Often they believe they have tried to warn people of their transgressions, to no avail, and therefore are driven to take violent action. The adult mass murderer will ruminate about the impending murder for days, weeks, or months. He or she will often prepare for the event meticulously and will spend the evening before the event fantasizing about the justice of finally getting even.

A mass murder will usually occur in one location, such as in an office, at a school, or on a campus. The perpetrators often kill themselves after completing their murderous "swan song." One such example is the 2007 Virginia Tech incident. The offender, Seung-Hi Cho, was a twenty-three-year-old student at the university; a resident alien from South Korea who had relocated to the United States as a boy. Cho had a history of mental illness and was described as a loner, withdrawn, and sullen. His grievance was with his wealthy and over privileged collegiate peers, whom he felt never understood him and rejected him.

He waited until the early morning of April 16th, knowing that Monday-morning classes would be well underway, and began the killing. Cho began his revenge seeking at a dormitory but eventually moved across the campus to the engineering building, Norris Hall. He made sure that many of the doors that would have served as exit routes were chained so that he could easily dispatch his victims as they realized they had no place to go. In the end, seventeen people were injured and thirty-three people were killed, including Cho, who took his own life. He did not want to be apprehended by authorities, another group of people who wouldn't understand him.

Spree Murder

Spree murder differs from serial murder with regard to motive. In one way, the objective may not necessarily be to prey on people but rather to obtain certain things such as a reputation, get away with robbery, gain immortality (nothing to lose), or get revenge against the establishment. The people who die at the hands of the spree murderer sometimes get in the way of an ongoing crime and become collateral damage during the commission of a crime, such as during a bank robbery or carjacking.

By the same token, the spree murderer may also be interested in killing others; he or she may feel that in some way, society has wronged him or her, and the opportunity to seek retribution is often through violence at multiple locations. These perpetrators do not try to keep their identity secret once the shooting starts. As suggested, spree murderers may move from one location to another and continue with the violent spree. During the commission of violence, this individual feels little or no remorse for the lives lost, while continuing on a quest to fulfill the need for revenge. For example, most Americans are familiar with the story of Bonnie and Clyde, another tragedy that Hollywood turned into an urban legend of sorts. Clyde Barrow and Bonnie Parker met in 1930 and participated together in a life of violent crime until law enforcement finally killed the two offenders in 1934. Bonnie and Clyde spent approximately two years engaged in a broad spectrum of activities ranging from car theft to robbery to murder to helping convicted felons escape from prison and throwing the occasional party after successfully escaping from law enforcement. Sometimes they killed people while getting away. Clearly, Bonnie and Clyde were sociopaths, with no regard for the rule of law, societal norms, regulations, or authority of any kind. They were two narcissistic predator perpetrators who believed that the possessions of others were available for the taking.

As with other types of murder, motives may vary among spree murderers. After the killing starts, spree murders appear not to have given much thought to escape, and many of them allow themselves to be taken into custody. At that point, they are open about their disregard for the law and eager to demonstrate their nonconformity and contempt, not only for the rule of law, but for individuals generally. Some of them want to be envied and admired, so they self-congratulate and self-glamorize; again this is one of the reasons they are often apprehended. For those individuals who are unfortunate enough to have happened upon the scene of a spree killing, they are treated no better than cannon fodder. Their deaths are simply useful in buying time. Many such victims are used as human barricades, considered necessary for the successful commission of a crime.

Some spree killers choose a location heavily and readily populated as a target-rich environment and engage in spree killing as a form of recreation. Their victims mean nothing to them. These killers enjoy watching the light go out of their victims' eyes.

People often ask why spree killers are so heartless about taking the lives of innocent people, or strangers who they have never seen before, whether their victims are young or old. To a spree killer, it makes no difference. However, one factor is clear: once the killing starts, there is no turning back. The killer is closed off to empathic feelings for others. This is true because of two vastly different emotions: empathy vs. murder. These emotions are not compatible and could not possibly be acted on together (simultaneously). If the killer had a conscience, the contrast between murderous action and empathy would be explosive, comparatively like two trains heading toward each other at a high rate of speed. As stated, the killer is closed off because caring and the desire to kill cannot coexist at the same time within the same human being.

Another reason why a spree killer will not show mercy to a former friend or acquaintance, or someone who has befriended him or her or shown a kindness, is because of that old saying, "Familiarity breeds contempt." A spree killer likely views kindness as taking pity on him or her. Oddly enough, that kindness perceived as pity could be the trigger for his or her outrage.

Spree killers show no mercy because they have rehearsed the violent acts in their minds and will act in accordance with their plans. As an example, I recall the death of a police officer who answered a call for service at a known ex-convict's home. A woman who said her boyfriend had beaten her placed a 911 emergency call. She informed the emergency 911 operator that her boyfriend ran out of the house with his rifle, and she watched him retreat into the forest. The deputy volunteered to take the call because he had known the perpetrator for several years and thought he could "talk him in." The dispatcher advised about the rifle, but the officer, a sergeant on the police force, was confident that the call would end as always, with the officer talking the perpetrator into surrendering and giving up his rifle. Other officers began to arrive at the scene and overheard the sergeant talking to a man hidden in the woods. They heard the man tell the sergeant, "You're not taking me in again." This statement was followed by a rifle shot to the sergeant's head. The point is, the killer had practiced his murderous thoughts until he became that killer he had been warning people about for years. It is interesting to note that the sergeant and the murderer had known each other since childhood and had been friends in school.

Conclusion

As we stated earlier, there may be resistance to a philosophy of self-reliance including self-protection. Some may argue about time expenditure weighed against return on investment. Others may be quick to say that mass murder does not happen often enough to warrant an alteration in one's thinking, or a change in one's habits, or they may say that there are overwhelming odds against a person being caught in such a tragedy. Our response is that even if that were true, are you willing to take that gamble and stake your life on it?

This chapter has presented a general overview to better understand the nature of a violent perpetrator. Such information is part of an education to improve dramatically the odds of saving yourself if caught in a violent incident. The truth is, violence is occurring right now. What guarantee does a person have that one's home, shopping center, or school will not be the next place where violence strikes? When a severe violent incident occurs, such as mass murder, it takes on a life of its own. Please refer to Appendix A to view the chart of characteristics of murderers.

CHAPTER 3

Proactive Observation

To increase your chances of surviving a violent event, we believe you need to understand how potential victims become engaged by violence and fail to use increased perception as a tool to enhance their chances of survival.

Sensing Violence

The precursors of violence are manifested in numerous ways. If you can pay attention to your surroundings with a heightened awareness, the five senses can often pick up an "undercurrent" warning that violence is at hand. However, to rise to the required reception level or the ability to receive the warnings, you must hurdle certain psychological obstructions; chief among these is the *denial barrier.*

In a psychological sense, denial is a defense mechanism employed by the superego structure so a person can resist the feeling of failing to be perfect. Denial also helps block out circumstances that could be dangerous or psychologically damaging. One way it works is to prevent us from noticing a disquieting disruption within the environment because we cannot tolerate it consciously. Therefore, denial works to prevent knowledge of elements that make a person very consciously uncomfortable.

Some stimuli that cause high or intolerable levels of anxiety include health problems, divorce, or violence. Humans may not be able to face these stimuli and therefore use denial as a method of channeling free-floating anxiety attacks. In this way, the anxiety takes precedence, becoming so distracting that a person cannot fixate on the source of the anxiety simmering beneath the surface. As a result, denial can prevent us from paying attention to warnings of impending violence.

For example, you may recall seeing on-scene interviews with people who have witnessed or survived a major calamity. Those people almost always say, "I couldn't believe it was happening" or "It felt unreal" or "I never saw it coming." Although denial certainly serves a purpose—for example, preventing people from feelings of failure or helplessness—we want you to override denial for the purpose of survival.

This strategy means you do not give yourself permission to ignore everyday activities going on around you, no matter what they are, where they are, or how irrelevant they seem.

In addition, survival strategy requires you to open up your unconscious thoughts, including genetic, intuitive, preprogramed abilities—elements that allow a person to receive survival messages. You should, for example, allow warning flags to be interpreted on your internal, personal radar screen. Although you may not be conscious of them, those warning signals are present; you are just not aware of them until you engage in consciousness-raising behavior.

Finally, it is necessary to reject the impulse to spring into action without understanding what you are doing and why. Ultimately, although denial is part of the ego protection system, it is not likely to help save a person's life in in the midst of a violent incident.

Personal Radar

A person's personal radar or early-warning system is composed of many organic elements, potentiated by a blend of cellular or biological components with social, cultural, and customary requirements. All of these components work together to prevent a surprise violent attack. Survival is one of the strongest of human drives, if not the strongest. This is not to say that everyone has the same level of effectiveness or efficiency, but the drive to survive is an instinct.

Ironically, like moths drawn to a flame, once violence has started, most people are inexorably drawn toward it until they are awakened to reality, which, by then, may be too late. In reality, we are being pushed by another, unconscious survival mechanism, which is the *information drive.*

Information Drive

Unfortunately for modern-day humans, the drive for information may push us into an inextricable situation. The information drive can be helpful if it operates in accordance with the rules of awareness for the sake of survival, rather than allowing it to push a person unconsciously toward danger. Some may call this the curiosity drive, but recall what happened to the curious cat.

People believe that if they become aware of a possible dangerous situation, the information drive that, when sublimated, changes an unacceptable thought or impulse into an acceptable form and becomes *unconscious curiosity.* The stronger this drive, the greater the potential for becoming ensnared and thereby stumbling into a violent incident. For example, think about day-to-day, ordinary violence and the reactions of people witnessing the violence, such as a building fire. Perhaps some of the witnesses simply become mesmerized by flames burning high, hot, and out of control. Caught up in the heat and leaping flames, they await, stupefied, for a chance to see flaming bodies running from a building or a house. Other spectators look on paralyzed, entranced by a disaster as it unfolds and comforted by the reassurance (as proof positive) that they are not experiencing flaming torment. Then there is a population of ambulance chasers who are determined to be the bearers of bad news. They cannot wait to share the gory details with willing listeners. They are spectators watching the dead and dying as the game of life plays out before their eyes. But such events offer some spectators a chance to be heroic, putting their lives at risk, helping the unfortunate victims. These are only a few unofficial groups engaged by violence.

Violence—the smell of it and the sound of it—naturally draws people toward it. As a former veteran patrol officer in the Dallas Police Department, I was responsible for training young, rookie officers on street patrol. Depending on the core nature of a trainee, some lessons were easy to teach, while others were not. I came to believe that some of the most difficult concepts and actions to train were modern-day survival behaviors. Those behaviors include how to react in the safest way, learn from each incident, practice thinking about such incidents, contemplate future variations of such incidents and their solutions, and prepare for a violent outbreak that could happen at any time by understanding that just because you have not been stricken by a violent incident does not mean you are somehow immune. More likely, it means that you are living on borrowed time.

For example, hearing gunshots nearby can spur one to spring into the wrong action, without thinking about the consequences and with no plan for the long or short run. Violent incidents are unforgiving, and wrong actions often equal death. Being ill-prepared may cause irreparable harm to an individual. We cannot afford to pay such a heavy price for being uninformed victims of violence.

A magnetism occurs within an event in which firearms have been discharged that initially leads people to gravitate toward gunfire rather than avoid it. Much like a rookie police officer, a person does not need to "run toward one's death" by failing to adhere to the rules of survival. Therefore, a few lessons are required about paying attention to danger.

For example, after a rookie's first shooting, shoot out, or near-death experience, that officer learns that it is best to perform in concert with the rules of survival. We hope you never have to face a violent incident, but if it should occur, it is possible to have a repertoire of survival actions you can engage in.

Perception Is Reality

Many are surprised to learn that the brain does not experience the world directly, but in fact, experiences the world indirectly through secondary information relayed by our senses. Sensation and perception are two psychological processes that operate in tandem. Sensation is any stimuli that the senses are sending to the brain to be processed, while perception is the brain's interpretation of that stimuli. For example, sound and color are constructs of the brain. That is, these interpretations of the environment do not exist outside of the brain. Sound is the brain's interpretation of vibration patterns in the air, while color is the brain's interpretation of a wavelength of light hitting the color receptors in the eye. The brain's perception of the environment is often based on expectations and past experiences. Consider that when police officers respond to a vehicular accident and ask witnesses to describe what occurred, the officers will receive various interpretations of the actual event. This occurs not because the witnesses are trying to be dishonest or misrepresent what occurred, but rather, the brain must selectively attend to information and is unable to process all incoming stimuli at one time. Fortunately for police officers, there is usually a kernel of truth in most witness accounts, a detail that remains consistent in all of the collective stories. A car accident is something that most people are familiar with; however, what if a person is witnessing or experiencing violence? If a person's brain has not experienced violence, or is hesitant to recognize an incident as violent, or simply in shock, that person may choose to take no action.

Seeing violence in action can be shocking and can cause even the most seasoned police officers, as well as citizens, to engage in unwise actions, such as failing to consider the consequences of each action based on real-time needs. For example, a rookie officer was on patrol in a neighborhood one evening as darkness closed in. A call came out for any police unit to respond to a woman who was screaming for help. Instinctively but wrongly, the young officer wanted to go to the front door to effect a rescue. Thank goodness the senior partner's experience prevailed. Both officers approached the house in question through the backyard. Peeping through a window on the west side of the house, they observed a man, later identified as the victim's husband, threatening his wife with a hunting-knife blade across the victim's throat, telling her how many ways he was going to slice her up. The rookie wanted to shoot him through the window, or at very least yell "Freeze! Police!" Fortunately, the senior partner put a restraining hand on his shoulder and signaled the rookie to follow him. Within moments, they had quietly gained entry through the back porch, from which they accessed the living room. The man was still swearing at his wife as he pushed the knife blade harder against her throat. The senior officer calmly but insistently announced, "Drop the knife, dead man." The perpetrator turned his head, looked at two pistols pointed at him, ready to kill him if necessary; he immediately complied.

Both husband and wife in the preceding example were intoxicated. The rookie later learned from the primary beat officer that about half the time, this couple traded roles, and the wife would hold her husband at gunpoint or knifepoint. Both had been arrested multiple times. Even a police officer in training needs to learn that things are not always what they appear to be. The rookie may have perceived himself to be a rescuer of women, failing to realize that women can also be the aggressors.

Think Smart and Be Smart

You may wonder how to make wise decisions about circumstances for which you have had little or no experience. It is the purpose of this book to provide readers with important methods of thinking, such as *active observation.*

Each of us is observing every day, deselecting or filtering out those items that are unimportant based on our level of awareness in combination with those factors considered important to us. Survival must be placed at the top of our list of important factors. It becomes a simple matter of raising consciousness. So how does a person raise consciousness? Let us revisit the Colorado theater mass murderer and take note of the following analysis. Remember that the movie was in progress. On the basis of what is known to this point, what question should theatergoers have asked themselves that evening, upon the appearance of the intruder? Why would an interruption be authorized by theater management while people are engrossed in a movie? That assumes that theater management and other theater employees are part of some elaborate charade that somehow fits into the movie experience. However, that kind of thinking does not make any sense at all. In reality, the intruder was acutely out of place; he had weapons, which made him dangerous, and audience members should have fled immediately.

Red flags were all over the place that would have caused an active observer to leave the theater. However, denial came into play. Anyone in that theater could have gotten up and walked out just before the shooting started, had it not been for *ambivalence caused by cognitive dissonance*. Some might argue that preemptive leaving may have been unjustified, but does that matter? It is not a big deal. Viewers could have gone back in the theater and reseated themselves if there had been no violent event.

Learning survival reasoning takes preparation. Furthermore, we believe that understanding factors that prevent survival-oriented thinking are just as important as knowing a general list of to-do behaviors. Human beings learn more effectively when they know the "whys and why nots," as opposed to being treated like children who have been given a list of commands to follow.

Most of us have a faulty belief that we are aware of our surroundings. This effect occurs due to the following:

- Ordinary familiarity, which should not be confused with awareness
- Years of surviving without being caught up in a violent calamity
- Not turning a discerning eye toward each environment we may find ourselves in

Most people who have attained adulthood have been unknowingly in danger, but awareness about it was below the level of a person's awareness threshold; perhaps the opportunity passed, and the person never knew what was about to happen. Most do not understand that each day, there is a field of land mines we must negotiate, and the fact that we do not blow ourselves up makes us believe we are safe. There are ongoing threatening activities within an environment that most are seldom aware of.

One of the main issues in training a new police officer has to do with awareness training. New police officers do not see what they need to see when first in training. They must be trained to look for the elements within circumstances that arouse attention. In other words, they have to be trained to become aware of circumstances that look wrong or out of place. Ironically, after a time, new police officers develop the awareness they need and become so focused on noticing what is wrong within their environment that they typically do not see or attend to things that do not prompt examination. The point is that becoming aware of one's environment has to be learned. Most people have learned to attend to circumstances that interest them. Unfortunately, that attention may not increase chances for survival.

Conclusion

So what does increased awareness really represent? You must become a proactive observer. By being proactive, you will learn to develop an early warning system for violence that will help you avoid becoming engaged by the violence to the point of inaction. Overriding the denial barrier is a key survival skill, as well as learning to have a raised consciousness about your surroundings.

CHAPTER 4

Proactive Prevention

ach day when we wake up, we turn on the news to see what new crisis we must face and add it to the list of intelligence we have already gathered. As bad news pours forth from the newsroom into our laps, many of us wonder what happened to our country; where did the good old days go? Some wonder if the "good old days" are ever coming back. Such wishes are fruitless, of course, because as time marches on and the good old days become a bygone era, a new era begins that requires adjustment to more frequent and varied displays of violence. Although many people are no longer surprised that this new way of living is permanent, they wonder how to maintain a sense of comfort and stability during such confusing and dangerous times. Within private moments, perhaps most people think about how to prevent violent events from happening, although recent efforts to stem the tide of violence appear to have failed, especially with regard to local, home-grown violence. Many wish to have a crystal ball to see when, where, and how a violent incident will erupt. But there are no crystal balls or any other tools that will tell us what to expect on any given day. Therefore, we are left with two main courses of action:

1. Passivity, wherein we stand by and become willing victims, or
2. Activism, wherein we become as prepared as possible for whatever comes down the road at any given moment. This level of readiness is described as becoming *proactive*.

A person can use preventive or proactive skills to avoid violent situations. To sharpen your skills, we will begin with how to gather intelligence during any ordinary day. Active observation includes hearing the warning signs and paying active attention to visual warning signals from others.

Active Observation

In ancient times, people would have no difficulty becoming *active observers*. Danger was all around humans, and not paying attention to subtle changes in the environment was likely a death sentence. For survival, ancient humans inherited the genetic predispositions to tolerate living in groups or tribes, which were the precursors of neighborhoods, towns, and cities. Our ancestors learned that survival was not possible if they were alone. Therefore, humans created communities to facilitate their security through banding together. Those individuals who attempted to exist outside the community would have little success finding a mate, food, or security. Outsiders would also miss out on daily social interaction. In addition, those individuals who were unable to contribute to the survival of the larger group, engaged in behavior that was counterproductive, or were deemed mentally and/or physically unfit would be eliminated or isolated from the greater society.

Today, humans make room for everyone. Those who would not have survived in ancient times are typically from the population that chose not to coexist within communities. They include the ones who did not fare well in society and those who acted in a destructive manner, such as sociopaths; mentally ill persons with violent tendencies; retribution seekers; people with delusions; and angry, hostile, conflictual, and aggressive people.

Gathering Intelligence

This is a talent and special skill we possess, although it varies from person to person. In other words, some people may not be as observant as others, which is one kind of inefficiency. Some people seem to draw the wrong conclusion more often than not. Luckily, this is not the case for the majority of people. Most people are more content when they feel up-to-date with the latest intelligence report, whether it is information about a relationship or a terrorist plot. We have evolved successfully from ancient times by being proactive, by "keeping a step ahead" with regard to potential or ongoing circumstances because a lack of knowledge would be disastrous.

This process is *intelligence gathering* or getting information. Sometimes we call the process other names, such as "the scoop," "the real skinny," "the 411," or "the status." Or we may simply ask, "What's happening?" No matter how we phrase it, it is indeed intelligence gathering. So for now, let's call it that. To take intelligence gathering a bit further, you must turn on and tune up your awareness mechanism and learn how to gather intelligence. This is an old but essential skill of human life, which begins with learning and using *focused listening skills*.

Deep Listening

Active observation is not a difficult activity to engage in, but it does take consistent work. A key component to active observation is listening to what people say. In the aftermath of violent attacks, people often come forward and reveal that the offender said or wrote things that caused some concern but were ignored. Consider the following quotes from violent people:

- "Natural selection needs a boost—like me with a shotgun."
  —Eric Harris, Columbine High School shooting (April 1999)
- "I would go crazy and kill all of the other teachers, and then I would painfully torture all of the principals to death."
  —Luke Woodham, Pearl High School shooting (October 1997)
- "You're all gonna die."
  —Andrew Golden, Westside Middle School massacre (March 1998)
- "We [referring to Muslims] love death more than you love life."
  —Nidal Hasan, Fort Hood massacre (November 2009)
- "I might as well kill myself."
  —Cho Seung Hui, Virginia Tech shooting (April 2007)
- "Don't you understand yet, you can't push me, and do you have any idea what I'm willing to do if pushed beyond what I'm willing to accept?"

> —Richard Farley in a letter to stalking victim Laura Black; workplace violence (February 1988)

- "When justified, terrorism is not necessarily a bad thing."
  —Djokar Tsarneav, Boston bomber (April 2013)
- "After I graduate, I'm going to Syria to join ISIS; I will be back someday to raise the black flag over the White House."
  —Student, Osbourn Park High School (October 2014)

The final quote, "After I graduate, I'm going to Syria to join ISIS (Islamic State of Iraq and Syria); I will be back someday to raise the black flag over the White House," is one of many comments made by a student attending a Northern Virginia high school in Manassas. This particular individual made a variety of sympathetic statements regarding ISIS and Islamic extremism over several months, to both peers and faculty members. For a period of time, both groups chose to ignore the remarks and engaged in a cognitive dissonance: "He doesn't realize what he's saying" and "He doesn't mean those things" or "He's saying those things to get attention."

However, it occurred to an employee of the school that there was a possibility that the student's statements were not benign, and perhaps the student meant what he was saying. After all, the student's peers had started complaining to faculty members about the inflammatory statements, which made them uncomfortable. The school employee made a decision to contact law-enforcement authorities and agreed to be interviewed about the student's statements. Law-enforcement officials found the student's statements and behavior so compelling that they interviewed many of the young man's peers, who also confirmed what the employee had reported.

Eventually, after months of surveillance, interviews, and intelligence gathering, it was discovered that this young man was a recruiter for ISIS and had helped another individual travel to Syria to join the extremist group. This young man was arrested on various federal charges pertaining to terrorism on February 27, 2015.

The lesson to be learned is that repeated statements about violence should be taken seriously because people may sometimes act upon their thoughts of violence. In short, people become what they think. In addition, the school employee did not overreact but acted as a collector and recorder of information so that the authorities were willing to investigate. In almost all of the instances of violence, in which a mass shooting has been the focus, those who claim familiarity with the perpetrator often recall a statement or action the individual made prior to the violent event. The neighbor, coworker, classmate, friend, or acquaintance realized that the statement or comment was in some way inappropriate, yet nothing was said or done in response. The response could be as simple as, "Do you really mean that?" or "Why are you saying that?" In some cases, the statement may be alarming enough to warrant a visit to authorities—law enforcement, a supervisor, a principal, etc. However, more times than not, people choose to ignore these statements and abandon deep listening. This is a mistake and causes severe regret among those who exercise complacency rather than diligence.

There are verbal descriptors of emotion that will help you determine whether there is a difference between what is called *simple anger* and *outrageous anger* that may lead to murder. People are continuously telegraphing what is on their minds, or what their intentions are, unconsciously. We believe that most of the time, people are getting the unconscious message, but because it is unconscious, the warning they are hearing is not registering. So it is important to define the cues you must become aware of to survive. The following chart identifies indicators of potential violence.

Verbal Indicators of Violence:
A Lethality Continuum

MILD	MODERATE	SEVERE
Feels treated unfairly.	Complains about instances of unfair treatment but takes no violent action.	Expresses outrage verbally and acts out against others.
Has no experience of injustice.	Perceives that injustice permeates daily life but is satisfied with complaints.	Perceives injustice and retaliates against those who have behaved unjustly.
Is angry but calm.	Not calm; anger expressed is directly disproportionate to perceived transgression (e.g., a "road rage" incident).	Is confrontational and creates conflict with others to release anger.

MILD	MODERATE	SEVERE
Is irritable/agitated.	Expresses agitation.	Is frequently and easily agitated.
Shows no verbal aggression.	Threatens physical aggression.	Engages in physical aggression with regularity (e.g., bar brawls, assaultive behavior).
Is not threatening.	Uses body, language, clothing, and possessions to project a threatening image.	Actively threatens others verbally and physically; relishes opportunities to instill fear in others.
Engages in light conflict.	Engages in periodic conflict.	Engages in constant conflict.
Does not induce anxiety.	Induces anxiety/discomfort	Enjoys causing anxiety/discomfort in others.
Is not enraged.	Is explosive, but rage extinguishes quickly.	Is explosive verbally and physically and shows a disregard for the safety and feelings of others.
Uses mild to moderate profanity.	Profanity increases.	Profanity is primitive sounding and used in socially inappropriate settings.
Organic verbiage is low.	Verbiage is crude.	Vulgarity is offensive.
Gesticulation is minor.	Gesticulation includes fist shaking, grabbing, pushing, etc.	Gesticulation rapidly becomes ranting.
Engages in sermonizing but no evangelizing, episodic but not routine.	Engages in evangelizing or frequent sermonizing.	Exhibits soap-box behavior or routine evangelizing.

Keying into the Meaning behind Clothing

We can learn much by paying attention to clothing; it reveals who we are, what we are, and what we believe. The Northern Virginia high school student we mentioned earlier who made the inappropriate statements in support of ISIS also revealed his true feelings using clothing. During his high school's spirit week, a five-day celebration in which the students dressed according to a theme, he decided to dress like an ISIS fighter.

The day he chose to do this was "America Day," when participants would wear the colors red, white, and blue to show their patriotism. However, this young man decided to arrive at school dressed like an ISIS militant. His outfit was carefully chosen so that there would be no mistake about his beliefs: black shirt, pants, camouflage military coat, black combat boots, and black scarf. His plan worked. His peers and some school employees took notice and reported the young man to the school administration. In this case, clothing paired with inflammatory comments clarified further what the young man's ideology was and perhaps what his intentions might be.

In addition, sometimes clothing identifies people who are dangerous, especially when we observe that the clothing is worn in conjunction with criminal acts or other such nefarious factors, such as in hostage taking (Patty Hearst and the Symbionese Liberation Army) or during a rally (the Aryan Nation, the Black Panther Party of the 1960s, or even the Ku Klux Klan). Clothing provides some people with a mechanism that helps distinguish them from the masses. You may recall that James Holmes, the gunman in the Aurora, Colorado, movie theater was dressed in a black uniform that resembled a law-enforcement-issued SWAT uniform. Eric Harris and Dylan Kliebold, who masterminded the Columbine High School massacre, were often referred to as belonging to the "trench-coat mafia," a group of misfit students who wore gothic clothing and long, dark trench coats. Seung Hui Cho, the individual responsible for the Virginia Tech shooting, created a video of himself before carrying out his plan, in which he was dressed in a paramilitary uniform, brandishing weapons, while ranting. Clothing or a uniform can set an individual apart from others or identify an individual as a part of a group. Oddly enough, identifying oneself as a group member gives a person status as an individual.

Visual Cues

It goes without saying that there are penalties for being unaware. One example immediately springs to mind: the mass shooting at a movie theater in Aurora, Colorado. According to one of the survivors of this incident, Jansen Young, she saw a man later identified as James Holmes appear in the theater dressed in a bizarre, black uniform. Young recalled noticing that the strangely dressed man threw something into the air, which landed behind Young and her date, John Blanc. The object was a tear-gas canister. At the time, Young believed the object was producing a smoke effect to enhance the patrons' movie-going experience.

When the man began to indiscriminately shoot the movie patrons, Young was experiencing cognitive dissonance and rationalized that the events were some kind of prank. It was not until her date, who had reacted to the violent attack by pushing Young down on the floor and shielding her with his body—a reaction likely prompted by Blanc's military training—that Young realized she was in the midst of a violent attack. Her boyfriend died shielding her from the gunfire, and when the shooting ended, Young remembered peering around a theater seat and telling her brain to "work" and find assistance for her boyfriend, whom she believed was seriously injured.

She managed to exit the theater only to find herself standing a few feet away from what appeared at first glance to be a police officer in SWAT gear. Young, now plugged into reality, was able to quickly discern that the individual standing with his back to her was the shooter, not a police officer. She proceeded to hide behind a metal Dumpster until the police found her and discovered that she was wounded.

In the above scenario, no one became alarmed until the perpetrator began tossing canisters filled with gas into the audience, followed by shooting people. No one concluded when first noticing his appearance that the man's behavior did not fit the environment. Unfortunately, the theater provided a "target-rich environment." After Holmes started killing people, the audience developed an awareness coupled with shock, and then the herding effect followed. The scene was a mess; the dead and wounded lay all around. People clogged the doors due to mass hysteria, which made a cluster target for the gunman; it would seem that people knew only how to panic.

Consider what individuals should have done. *Active observation* requires that you become as conscious as possible of all things happening around you while deselecting or filtering issues by level of importance at the moment. For example, Jansen Young fell into a state of cognitive dissonance. According to Leon Festinger (who coined the phrase "cognitive dissonance"), "In a state of dissonance, people may sometimes feel disequilibrium: frustration, hunger, dread, guilt, anger, embarrassment, anxiety, etc." Thus, individuals in this state will seek to reduce the feeling or anxiety that the dissonance produces by altering their views, belief system, or opinions.

Initially, Young was convinced that the situation as it unfolded was an elaborate joke she was not privy to. A person must learn to prioritize and attend to those things of greater probable value to survival. Young was able to do this only after realizing that her boyfriend had been shot. She concluded that she must exit the theater and seek help. In this new state of mind, Jansen was able to recognize that the man was carrying too many weapons and was not engaged in law-enforcement practices such as assisting injured patrons, and he was out of place. Once hypervigilant, Young was able to correctly understand that she should conceal herself and avoid further confrontation with the perpetrator.

Skills to Employ in a Violent Situation

Let's start by examining one of the environments you may find yourself in when violence erupts—for example, a college campus. If you are attending a college or university, you should become aware of the physical environment of the campus. To accomplish this, it will require time to familiarize yourself with the campus grounds. It will entail imagining what you would do if a violent incident broke out in every part of the campus where you might be present. Developing an awareness of good places to take cover is a key skill for survival.

Cover and/or Concealment

You must know the difference between *cover* and *concealment*. Cover implies not only that you cannot be seen, but that projectiles cannot penetrate the cover you are hiding behind. For example, a hedgerow would provide concealment but not cover. Basic to survival in a violent incident is exploring the environment and noting particular places that could offer potential cover or concealment.

A motor vehicle is not the best choice for cover; however, if it appears to be the only possible cover, use it. If it is the best option, avoid lying down on the ground parallel to the vehicle due to bullet skipping. *Bullet skipping* occurs when a projectile strikes a hard surface, such as blacktop or cement, at even a slight angle. The projectile will follow its original course of trajectory, a few inches above the surface, until the projectile or bullet loses inertia. This same principle holds true even if you are on a sidewalk or parkway, encased by a hard-surfaced curb, such as cement. If a round has been skipped on the street, in the direction of the side of a car, the projectile rises a few inches above the surface of the street, passes under the car, and strikes the curb, running parallel with the car. Provided the projectile still has energy when it strikes, it will bounce upward, between the curb and the car. The result to someone who may be leaning against the car in line with the projectile could prove fatal.

The same effect occurs with projectiles that strike a hard-surface wall at an angle. I witnessed one person lose his nose when he peeked around the corner of a building. He had taken cover on the side of the building, away from the gunfire. When he took an extended look around the corner, he lost his nose and part of his face. Consider *prairie dog peeking* as an alternative.

Prairie-Dog Peeking

This technique requires the person who needs to gain visual intelligence to change the height of viewing from one peeking position to another, without establishing a pattern. Consider that the process of peeking is similar to viewing a series of photos taken of a subject in motion, but at different angles so that the viewer gets a different perspective. You should never peek around a corner or obstruction at the same height twice. Vary the position of your body to gain a visual perspective of what is happening around you.

Escape Routes

If you attend to your environment before violence occurs, then you should already have a cognitive map of possible escape routes in place. There should always be more than one escape route available because your first option may be too close to the violent event. For example, in the Virginia Tech shooting, and specifically within Norris Hall, Cho had chained the exit doors so that immediate escape would not be possible for his victims; fortunately, some students were cognizant of the fact that many of the classroom windows could be opened and used as a means of escape.

Don't Become a Pop-Up Target

Emotions run high both during and after a violent incident; law-enforcement officers and others remain on alert, even after the incident is seemingly over. It would be tragic if officers failed to find a culprit who had not been flushed out, and then the perpetrator killed someone after the incident had been declared over. Therefore, one of the most dangerous periods for survivors is between incident resolution and the withdrawal of authorities. When guns are involved, anything can happen, including death as a result of friendly fire. If you get caught in the midst of a violent incident and find a place to hide, it is vital to *not* become a pop-up target. In other words:

- Never pop up quickly or abruptly emerge from concealment.
- If you have materials with you, do not stand up with items in your hands. For example, if there is a bomb threat, do not emerge from concealment with a briefcase in hand; that kind of accessory might put you in danger.
- People are often reluctant to throw down their things while attempting to escape or seeking cover. Leave them lying in place until you can get permission to retrieve them. When the police determine that no further threat exists, you will be able to retrieve your items.
- When the time is appropriate, let the police know of your hidden presence.

- Call out to police officers in a loud voice and say, "Police officers, I am over here!" Continue to make that statement at regular intervals until someone in authority responds to you. Remember that law-enforcement officers will not know who you are.
- You must do everything they say until they can clear you and determine that you are not a threat.
- Do not become angry if it takes a while for the police to find you. It is in your best interest to keep your cool, follow directions, and let the events unfold as they should.
- You will be treated as a potential culprit until they can clear you. They may make you show your hands, ask you to lie prone on the ground, and treat you like a suspect. Do not become indignant, argue, or protest with statements like, "I didn't do anything!" They will discover that for themselves, and you will be secured. Until that time, the police will not harm you or let you be harmed while you are in their custody. The authorities will appreciate your cooperation and remaining calm instead of behaving hysterically or indignantly.

Conclusion

It is important that you learn the skills for proactive prevention. In this way, you will have time to assess your environment, listen for inappropriate statements, and look for odd behavior. If you find yourself in a violent situation, employ these survival skills: Take cover or seek concealment, assess the situation using prairie-dog peeking as a means to gain visual intelligence about the perpetrator and your surroundings, and most importantly, recognize possible escape routes.

CHAPTER 5

Commitment to Stay Alive

Most of us are inadequately prepared for meeting the challenge presented by a spontaneous, violent incident. It is not that we have received inadequate parenting, but that most of our parents did not know what to tell us about violence. Therefore, most of us entered adulthood with little more than general knowledge about violent incidents, and perhaps rightly so, because there is no reason to upset children unnecessarily. The vast majority of people in this country are not exposed to violence with enough regularity to necessitate survival training in their upbringing. Even those raised in neighborhoods in which there are frequent drive-by shootings and other forms of violence are only slightly better prepared for an up-close and personal, face-to-face incident with a mass murderer.

But life is changing radically in the United States. To survive, we must adapt quickly. Long past are the days in which neighbors kept each other informed on the status of their communities, whether at the office or over the backyard fence. Nowadays, our neighbors are not our friends; more likely, they are strangers with whom we have little or no communication, which is another unfortunate aspect of our changing, transient society.

The newest phenomenon to take hold of Western society is that we are instructed by electronic media when we should take extra precautions if an alert status changes. Today's color-alert status may be for the likelihood for a terrorist attack, or that the pollen count is high, so stay indoors. However, an alert for mass murder today will not be given. So what do you do if you are at a shopping center and someone starts shooting? If the truthful answer is "I don't know what to do" or "I would call the police" or "I would leave it up to mall security," then this book will teach you skills that will help you become a survivalist.

It is safe to say that positive effects from making decisions about life's important issues come down to having made sound, effective choices. Most of us go through life without experiencing disastrous events and therefore conclude that we must be making great decisions. The truth is, for the most part, no one is challenging the decisions we make, which leaves us with the false impression that "I can manage whatever circumstances I am confronted with." More accurately; however, we should become aware that people tend to make better decisions about circumstances they are most familiar with. Surviving violence may depend on how committed a person is to adapting by becoming familiar with unpleasant and dangerous circumstances. As stated earlier, success or failure often depends on whether or not, at any given moment, a person makes the right choice.

We hope you will never be faced with a situation in which you must make a dramatic or drastic choice to save your own life. However, logically and intuitively, we know that a bad situation can arise right out of the blue. One moment, the course of your life is proceeding without event, just as would be expected. You march off down life's highway, basking in the sun as you encounter ordinary challenges that bring forth ordinary concerns, some of which cause no more than surface worry and anxiety. Then "Bang!" Clouds move in, and the heavy rain starts instantly. Caught with no raincoat and no cover, you may worry about your hair or clothes getting wet. But when it's raining bullets, a whole different perspective on life emerges. Depending on what you do, there may be no tomorrow, no story to tell about making it or overcoming adversity. If you are committed to survival, then it is important to look at how awareness fits into the picture.

Individual Awareness

Awareness plays a big part in the picture of survival. We all need to be committed to survival or being willing to learn new information, apply it, and use it appropriately and also forgo bad habits born of illogical, unreasonable, and invalid information, training, and thinking. In other words, we must be open to new ideas and the practical application of survival methods. Awareness becomes a way of life; it does not present a hardship in the sense that being aware is an unnatural process. Awareness means that the world opens up like a fourth dimension, allowing us to see what others do not see. Awareness helps us shape the instinct to survive or facilitate a more effective use of our senses by using goal direction.

Although awareness has a starting point from which we begin, awareness is also a perpetual process that does not end. For example, one factor of awareness has to do with noticing our environment. One aspect of "noticing" has to do with looking around and "assessing" what we are seeing. In so doing, we might take into account the cover available should a shot ring out. We might also take into account any avenues of escape and avoid blind alleys or what is referred to as a "death trap." Improved awareness might mean taking the time to survey a regularly traveled environment, such as a campus route or university buildings frequented for classwork, and become visually familiar with entrances and exits, death traps, and emergency means of escape. It is not enough to assume that "those doors" lead outside. If those doors for one reason or another are not accessible, what is plan B? Your life is worth putting in the time required to become aware and to make it a habit. Again, choices make a difference. But how do you make a smart choice? Smart choices or decisions may be the deciding factor between life and premature death.

Relying on Peers

No matter how independent we may be, we are all susceptible to peer pressure. This kind of pressure often comes in subtle forms, such as the way we groom ourselves or the kind of clothing we wear, according to our age or other status. We ask each other about popular movies to see or restaurants to eat in. There are some ways in which we, as individuals, seem independent, but fundamentally, when fear comes into play, we are likely to act more like sheep, following along, doing what appears to be the right thing—for two reasons.

First, we notice that everyone else is doing it, so it must be right. Second, having no other familiar option, we will follow because if others seem to know what to do and we don't, then they must be right. Once that process takes place, which is almost instantaneous, abandoning that faulty decision is unlikely. Because the decision was based on an instinctual wish to survive, any activity counter to that decision will register as wrong. To put it another way, *cognitive dissonance* would set in.

It is one thing to address theory and some psychological ideas, but the need to know specific means of acquiring and becoming proficient in Survival Skills Self Training (SSST) is important.

In the beginning of this book, we stated that a person does not need to have special skills such as boxing, wrestling, karate, jujitsu, or any other kind of martial arts. That is because the most important skill is to be open to a new way of thinking, including the ideas contained here. Specifically, survival in a violent incident demands the following:

- Relying on yourself as the first most effective line of defense
- Spending considerable time practicing recommended new skills
- Staying alive until professional help, the police, and other emergency services arrive to assist you

In this chapter, we explain how to engage in self-training. You will practice needed skills to become comfortable and proficient in their use. The process is circuitous, with success building on success.

It is important to understand the rules for developing self-taught skills. Following directions will build proficiency and confidence slowly. Skipping a skill in the instructions may result in injury. Going forward with practicing the skills that need to be developed will highlight strengths and weaknesses as the difficulty factor is increased.

Time is required to engage in self-training. Some of the aspects of self-training are of particular interest because they require a person to watch people in various environments. Keep in mind that in no way are we suggesting stalking another person because he or she is interesting. Still, there is no reason why one cannot observe people and their behavior, whether at a shopping mall, work, or school. For example, noticing bumper stickers can convey a lot of knowledge about the owner of the car, and the way people dress and groom themselves can convey important information for a trained observer.

We refer to our form of training as *method training*. Requirements may seem demanding, but with practice you will become skilled. Within a few weeks, you will find that you can spontaneously perform skills to stay safe. In addition, you will begin to notice things in the environment that you did not see before because they seemed irrelevant.

Skills to Learn

Cover and concealment

First, you will need to improve your ability to identify cover and concealment opportunities, places that will essentially help you hide and avoid becoming a victim of violence, no matter where you are. Pay particular attention to the factors that constitute cover and concealment later in this chapter.

Extrication from a danger zone

Again, as soon as possible, try to find a means of escape while a violent incident is still unfolding. The longer you wait, the more likely the scene is to become more entrenched with regard to violent action. Military personnel who were trained in guerrilla warfare prior to deployment to Vietnam were taught counterinsurgency. They learned that if they were caught by the enemy, the best time to escape is as soon as possible. The longer you wait to extricate yourself, the greater the level of entrenchment, which means all participants begin to play their part in concert with the circumstances of capture. In other words, if you think of yourself as a captive, you will indeed become a captive; the power of the situation has a direct effect on attitudes.

Consider the case of the Stanford Prison Experiment, organized by Dr. Philip Zimbardo in 1971 at Stanford University. In the experiment, which Dr. Zimbardo intended to last only two weeks, he discovered that people quickly become what they thought. Dr. Zimbardo screened male participants, who were students at Stanford University. Half of the participants were randomly selected to play the role of a prison guard, while the other half were selected to play the role of a prisoner. The guards were given uniforms of khaki shirts, pants, mirrored sunglasses, whistles, and nightsticks, while the prisoners were made to wear plain white gowns and caps, and were given identification numbers.

Within a twenty-four-hour period, and without prompting, both the guards and prisoners decompensated and began to act in accordance with their prescribed roles. Forty-eight hours later, the role playing was extreme. The prisoners came to believe that they could not leave the basement of the psychology building at Stanford University; they believed they were truly imprisoned. The guards began abusing the prisoners for their own amusement. Over a period of six days, the guards made the prisoners perform demeaning and degrading tasks such as cleaning the toilets with their bare hands and playing leap frog. Most of the prisoners became complacent and indulged the guards to avoid further punishment.

What is disconcerting about this experiment is that both groups of participants could have quit the experiment at any time and would have received pay for two weeks of participation, regardless. However, only two prisoners quit the experiment, and those individuals felt guilty about leaving the remaining prisoners. Dr. Zimbardo stopped the experiment after six days. For more information about this experiment and similar cases, read *The Lucifer Effect* by Philip Zimbardo, PhD.

Preventive action

In keeping with the above recommendations regarding extrication from the violent location, we recommend practicing escape and evasion. Such preventive action begins with this thought: *What would I do if...?* This kind of training requires you to scout out places you go frequently and to develop a plan for survival, including an escape route from each of those places. Training yourself by thoughtfully assessing environments that are familiar will greatly enhance your ability to identify what action will be needed in locations that are not familiar to you.

Intelligence gathering

Intelligence gathering via reconnoitering (recon) is what we suggest when scouting out familiar places, as well as locations you are unfamiliar with. To carry out intelligence gathering, a person will rely on certain ancient personality traits, as well as expansive new concepts. This will require you to become a silent observer, wherever you may find yourself.

Our hearing becomes finite when we recognize sounds we are familiar with. We should become alert when we hear sounds we are not familiar with rather than ignoring them. Sounds that put us on alert are part of the groundwork for survival. Lower animals listen for danger and sniff the air; however, humans have come a long way from attending to those ancient senses. But there's nothing that prevents us from regaining ground with regard to our ability to sense trouble. Therefore, begin attending to the noises in your surrounding environment. Learn to compare familiar sounds that you would expect to hear, and become acutely alert when you hear unfamiliar sounds. Under the right circumstances on the basis of hearing unfamiliar and disturbing noises, a person should act quickly and decisively with regard to safety issues. Again, this requires awakening the senses. Even though you may not be the target, perpetrators will likely not hesitate to dispose of you to prevent you from becoming an obstacle in their path.

A few words about physical fitness

One key aspect of survival is being physically fit. Developing stamina, strength, and coordination will help you endure the challenges of a violent incident. Maintaining a high fitness level may allow you to sustain a rigorous attack for approximately thirty seconds. It is recommended that you try to engage in thirty minutes of exercise each day.

If you have poor coordination, it will take longer for you to learn how to be more physically balanced while developing the musculature support you need to accomplish your physical goals. We stress the importance of taking time to learn what your body can do and what it does not do well and then work on improving those areas of weakness.

For example, getting up and out of a rolling chair can be a challenge. To compensate, you may be off-balance trying to stand up and move forward at the same time. Imagine the multiple outcomes from such a move. Practice getting up ordinarily and move toward the door to exit a space. Now increase your speed and notice how awkward it is to crouch forward and rise from the chair without the chair shooting backward and out from under you. You may want to practice this move with a close friend or partner who tries to prevent you from trying to get to the door after a few seconds.

If you sit behind a desk, avoid hitting the desk corner with your hip or abdomen. The same kind of exercise can be employed with a regular, straight-back chair. To become proficient with these skills, practice them over and over until they become second nature.

In a crisis situation, panic is the enemy because it keeps a person from being surefooted. The mind will likely be focused only on the necessity of getting up and out; however, it is necessary to remain calm to get out of an office without damage to yourself. If you work in an office, become aware of sharp edges on furniture or objects that could be harmful if you are trying to run to safety. Also, become aware of items you could use to assist in the escape.

It is also important to be prepared for an assault on your body by understanding what an involuntary push/shove feels like and what it is like to struggle with an assailant on the floor. First, never stop moving during the assault or attack while on the ground or floor, or if your attacker tries to pin you against a wall. Continue to resist by turning your body; you're not down until you're unconscious or dead. A phone book or its equivalent is an effective blocker against punches—find one and keep it near you in your home or work space.

Most people are not used to being assaulted or in physical fights. Therefore, the first time you are hit in the face, it will stun you. In fact, you can become stunned into a mental paralysis. To offset such a reaction, we urge you to become familiar with some practiced assault behaviors. Ask a friend or spouse to very softly push you, with the palms of his or her hands placed against the front of your shoulders, while your back is positioned against the wall. The friend should gradually increase the force but not injure you. This is just practice to get you familiar with what it feels like to be struck or held in place. Practice struggling around the wall so that if you are in contact with edges of furniture or other uncomfortable objects, you will be ready. The whole scene will seem foreign to you.

A final exercise is to find an old duffel bag. You may have to go to the army-navy outlet store to find one. Fill the bag with as much clothing as you can to make it as heavy as possible. Then get down on your knees and wrap both arms around the bag, as if you are giving it a bear hug. Very carefully practice rolling around on the floor. Every time you practice, start out slowly, with very measured activities, and work toward increasing your tolerance and skill level. However, if you find that you are unable to engage in an exercise, stop trying to accelerate the pace and return to the most comfortable level of practice.

Understanding the Curve

The *curve* describes a visual field in which victims become targets, or they find themselves in the assailant's direct line of vision or in the direct line of fire at an indoor or outdoor event.

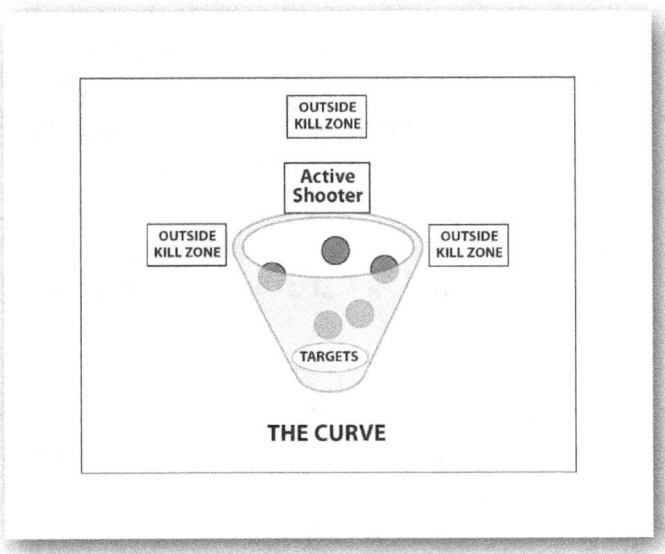

THE CURVE

Look at the diagram and notice where the curve sits on the funnel. The perpetrator stands at the widest point of the funnel and prevents the victims from escaping by filling the kill zone with gunfire. If you are trapped in the kill zone of an active shooter who is shooting right to left or left to right in a sweeping motion, move in the opposite direction of the sweep, which places you outside of the curve. The shooter's objective is to have as many targets as possible by drawing them into the narrow part of the funnel. Do not be drawn into this area.

Once you are outside the curve, the shooter has to make an instantaneous decision to discontinue firing at multiple targets within the kill zone to shoot at you. Once you are outside the kill-zone area, seek out cover or concealment in one of the places you previously identified. Remain aware of the shooter's location so that you can move and escape the environment entirely. By not freezing up, fleeing the kill zone, and seeking cover/concealment, you have increased your chances of survival.

Inside/Outside Events

To help you understand various scenarios in which violence may occur, we have presented some examples of the types of incidents you may be caught in. We have classified those incidents into two large categories: *inside environmental incidents* and *outside environmental incidents.* Incidents occurring in an inside environment might be those in a classroom, an office, a theater, a shopping mall, or other contained areas. Violence occurring in an outside environment may be in a park, a neighborhood backyard, a parking garage, entering or exiting an office building, or on a college campus. No matter where you are, you must remain aware of activities in your immediate environment at all times, even if the surroundings seemingly offer no reason to be concerned.

To summarize, here are the general strategies for increasing safety in an incident:

- Become completely aware of your environmental surroundings.
- Know the floor plan/design of your immediate environment, which includes adjacent hallways, bathrooms, conference rooms, maintenance closets, exits, and entrances.

- Develop a safety plan that revolves around the most defensible positions or hiding places.

We have provided a series of diagrams for the purpose of assessing and recognizing escape scenarios. Although there is not a foolproof way to survive a shooting, these suggestions will help you increase your survival skills by becoming aware of your surroundings and determining escape strategies by using visual and auditory skills.

Specific Inside Events

The diagrams in this section will give you a chance to assess a situation and recognize preventive actions that you can implement prior to or during a shooting.

Large office

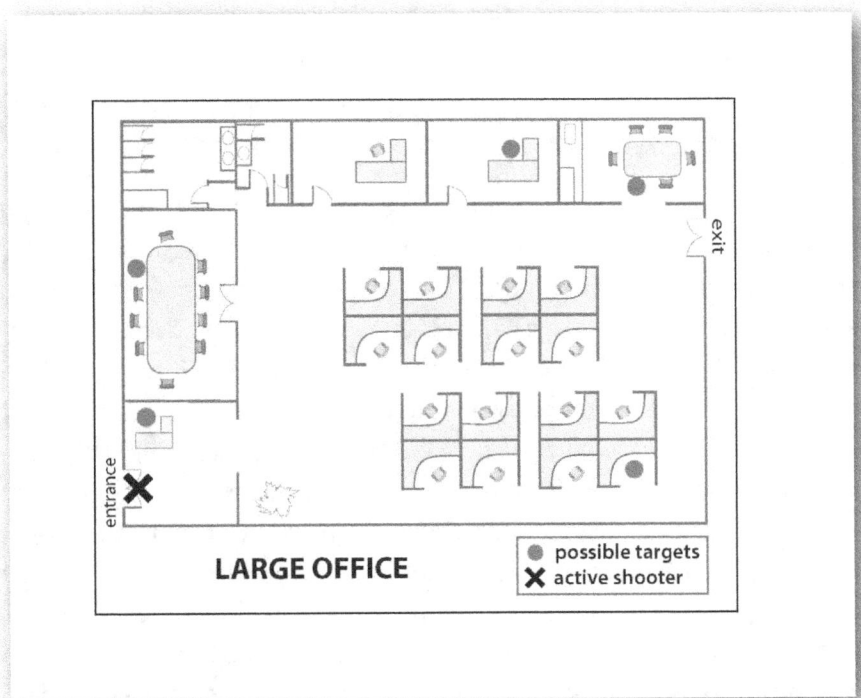

Based on the above situation in this large office, imagine you are one of the possible targets and the shooter is located at the entrance. Assess the situation and determine the possible choices you would make to survive. Remember to avoid the shooter's curve.

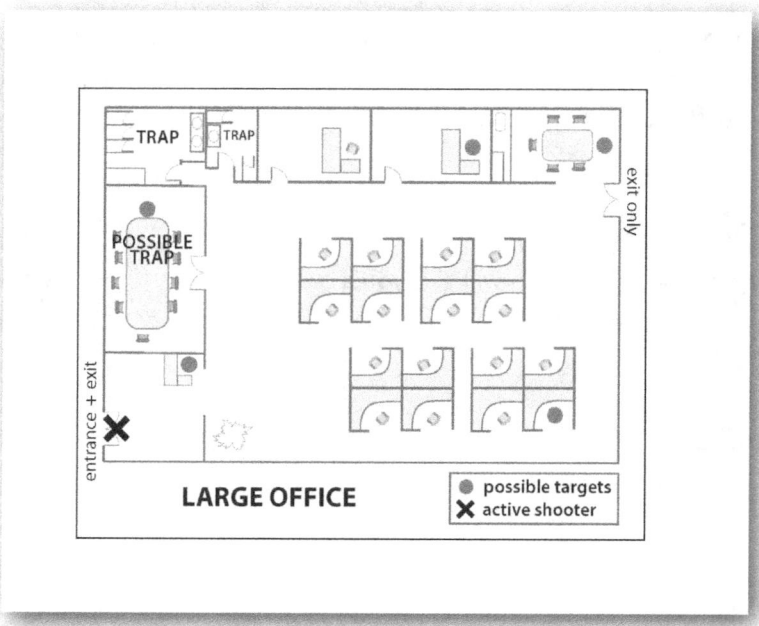

Looking at the same large-office diagram, you will notice that changes have been made to improve the safety of the workers. First, notice the doorway. It is recommended that there is only one entrance clients and guests can use to enter the space. However, the other entrances and exits can be used to exit the office from the inside. There is now only one way into the office instead of two. This allows office workers to develop one plan instead of two for escape. Second, notice where the possible targets are now sitting. They are no longer in the direct line of fire and have a better chance of escaping, whether it is through the exits or by barricading a room. It is important to recognize that the conference room is a trap because there is only one exit. If you attend a meeting, you should sit close to the door but out of the direct line of fire. When shots are first heard, get out of the room and head to the exit. If this is not possible, shut and lock the door and try to barricade yourself inside the conference room with heavy furniture. Notice in this diagram that the receptionist desk has been moved. This will give that individual a better chance of escape around the wall and out the back exit.

Learn to listen for unusually loud noises. There is a difference between the sound of a firearm being discharged and, for example, a firecracker. Listen for the sounds of people in distress, such as cries for help. If you can determine from the cries that there is an invasive, dangerous person in close proximity, then act on a predesigned plan for escape. The predesigned plan may include using an emergency exit or moving to a room where you remain out of sight. However, if unsure about where the danger is in relation to your position, take caution. Stay low and listen again for voices, cries for help, the discharge of a firearm, and other atypical noises. Make sure that any movement is purposeful and takes you away from, not toward, the noises.

Small office

Two diagrams have been created with visible differences. Study the two diagrams to consider why the changes were made.

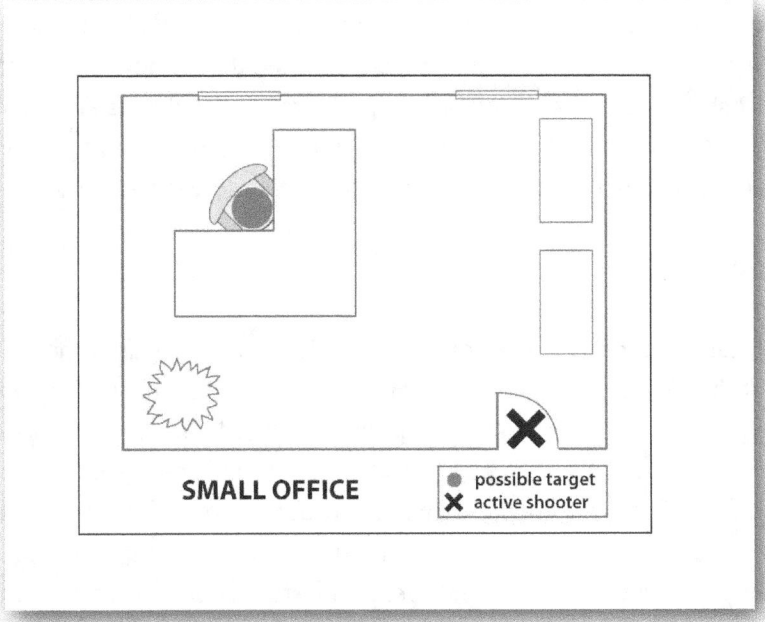

SMALL OFFICE

● possible target
✖ active shooter

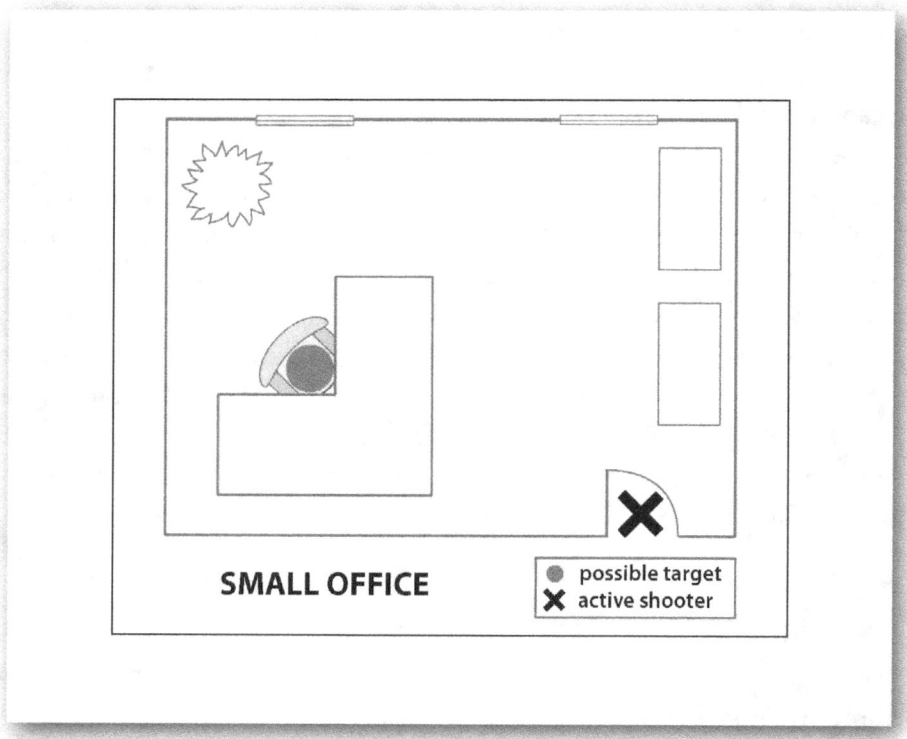

SMALL OFFICE

● possible target
✖ active shooter

Notice in this diagram how the desk has been moved closer to the south wall. By placing it there, the person occupying the desk is not in the direct line of fire. If shots are heard in the hallway, the first line of defense is to shut and lock the door. Then, if there is time, the worker can use the filing cabinets to barricade the door. He or she can then use the window for escape.

Schools

School staff practice lockdown procedure drills regularly; while some educators feel that drills are a waste of time because instructional time is lost, in moments of ambiguity, people default to training. In other words, one should always practice safety. Teachers and students who know of individuals in their respective educational buildings who are not complying with lockdown drill procedures have an obligation to report this to administration. Practice can improve one's ability to survive a violent incident. The students and staff deserve this opportunity.

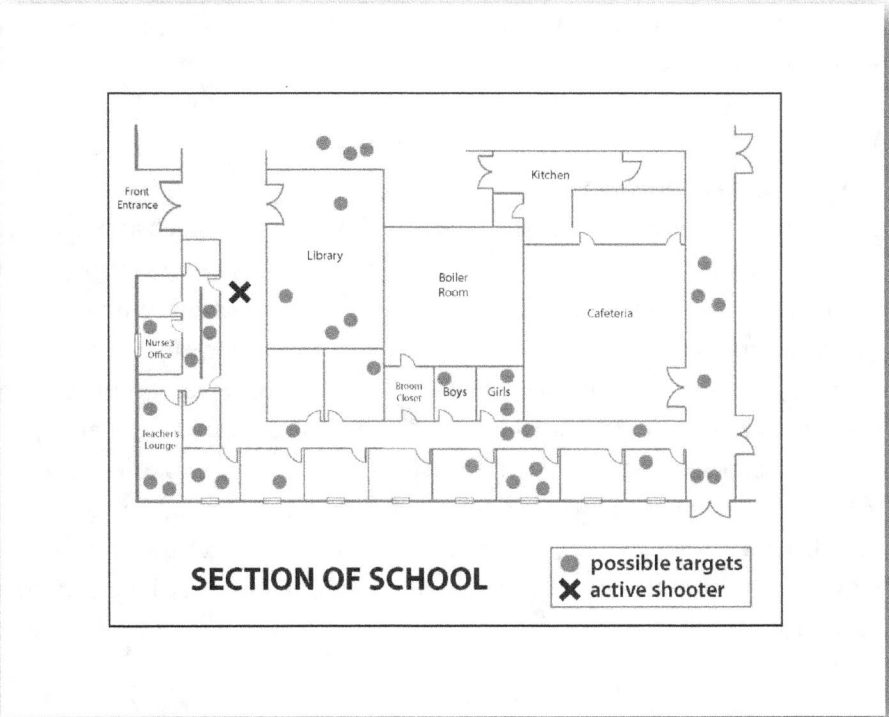

SECTION OF SCHOOL

● possible targets
✖ active shooter

If students or staff members are outside a classroom and hear unusually loud noises, such as a firearm discharging, they should use prudent caution in returning to the assigned classroom. They should try to discern from which direction the noises originated and decide whether to stay where they are and seek cover in a closet or other concealed area that has already been scouted out, or return to the classroom. This book requires that people come to grips with tough decisions, and that is why preplanning is important. If a student is out of the classroom in the midst of a violent assault on the school, the teacher will not let him or her back inside the classroom because teachers are responsible for those who are already locked in the room.

Educators and students have a responsibility to help school safety personnel keep the building secure. This means that if they see an individual who looks out of place, they should report it immediately. In addition, during the school day, educators and students should not feel obligated to let individuals into the building through doors that are not designated as secured entrances; instead, they should remove themselves from that location/entrance area and proceed to the main office to report the incident.

Target-rich environments

Educational facilities often create target-rich environments such as pep rallies, the cafeteria, the auditorium, the gymnasium, the library, moving through the hallways between classes, etc. Another target-rich environment within a school is one where the perpetrator creates one. During an attack, the intruder might engage the fire alarm. This allows the shooter an opportunity to open fire as the students exit their classrooms and the building. If an attack is confirmed, teachers and students must wait for fire or police officials to arrive to save those in the building from attack. Do not let a panicked teacher or students override training; do not open the door or leave the area of safety. Again, we stress that success will depend on one's forethought and practice in assessing the situation and developing a plan to help survival chances.

Arming teachers

There is a movement in regions of the United States to arm teachers as a means of bolstering security, much like arming commercial pilots following 9/11. We have concerns about arming teachers in educational settings, even though they may be receiving excellent firearms training. They need combat training as well. Even the most seasoned police officer will tell you that engaging in combat training takes intensified training over an extended period of time. There is no evidence that teachers who have been armed have received the kind of combat training that is necessary.

In the midst of a crisis, the most valuable skill is the ability to communicate effectively with other "friendlies" to avoid friendly fire. Police officers would call this a *blue-on-blue incident*. In the 1960s, police officers conducted "cotton-bullet" training. The firearms were loaded with cartridges, which were filled with color-dyed cotton, so that officers could identify who shot whom during the training scenarios. In the scenarios, it was discovered that police officers were more likely to shoot one another, rather than the intended target, principally because of poor communication. We believe the most effective method for keeping people safe in an educational environment is to provide training on how to protect oneself without arming teachers.

Theater

Recently, theaters have become a target-rich environment for those seeking notoriety. Below are two examples showing where you might sit within a theater: either on the aisles or in the middle. You should always note where the exit doors are in the theater, and if possible, sit near an exit. It is advisable to arrive early to your movie of choice so that you may choose your seats, rather than accept the seating that is left. In fact, if there are so many patrons attending the same film that you are unable to choose your seats, then choose not to see the movie on that particular day.

If the exit doors on either side of the film stage remain secured, most shooters will enter from the back of the theater, which is also the main entrance for patrons.

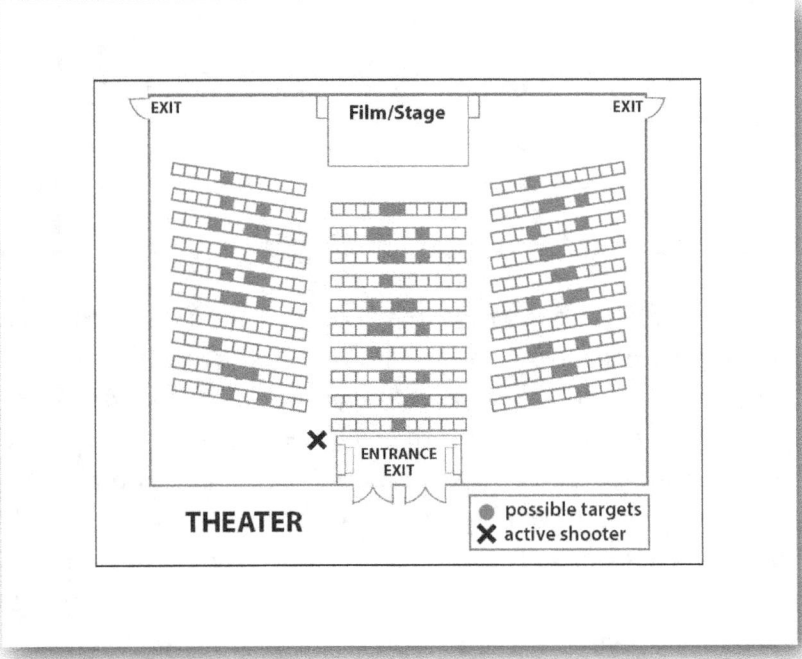

We urge you to avoid sitting in the middle of a row because this impedes your ability to extricate yourself from a violent situation and lessens your chances for survival dramatically. Your best line of defense in this scenario will probably be cover and concealment from the seats. By climbing over the seats, you make yourself a target.

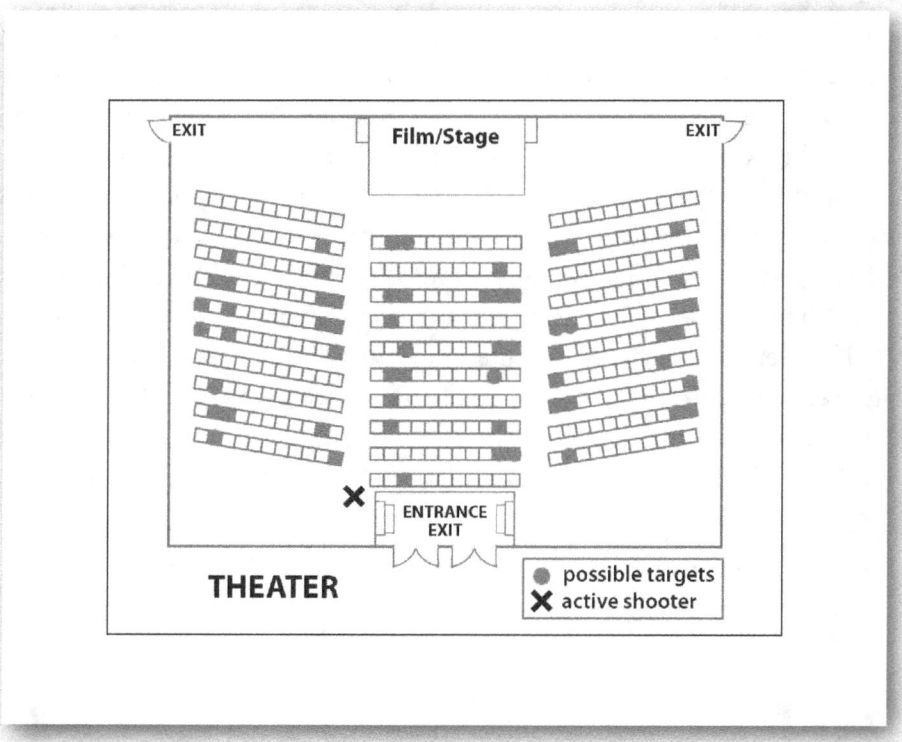

Select a seat located in one of the aisles and close to an exit; should a violent shooting occur, you want to get out first. Remember that people will engage in the herding effect and begin to clog the rows and exits as they attempt to escape, so avoid the curve. However, if you are not able to reach an exit safely, use the darkness of the theater and the seats for cover/concealment. Move along the theater floor slowly and quietly; use the prairie-dog peeking skill to locate the shooter. Continue to move away from the shooter slowly until you are able to reach an exit or find better cover or concealment.

Specific Outside Events

Again, we offer a series of diagrams to help you understand survival strategies in a variety of open, public spaces.

Public Parks

COMMUNITY PARK

● possible targets
✖ active shooter

The survival strategies to use in public parks are simple and logical. First, you should become aware of all possible exits out of the park. Try to get to the street, where you can take cover behind cars or get help from a person driving on the street. If trees are present, use them as a line of defense as well. Do not follow everyone else trying to escape because it creates a target-rich environment for the shooter, with many people clustered together.

Parks do present some obstacles. For example, many parks are surrounded by chain-link or other kinds of fencing. Objects for recreational use in the park that are provided for children can present navigation difficulties in the event of a shooting. It will be easier to protect yourself if you remain on the periphery rather than in a position that is potentially in the middle of the situation.

Although parks are considered places of fun and recreation, you must practice the skill of observation to avoid being victimized by a random spree shooting. Again, the strategies of stop, look, and listen come into play. Become habituated to observing the surroundings periodically and making note of activities or people who do not appear quite right. A park is a place of easy access and easy egress. So it is important to establish a plan in case violence erupts, noting routes of escape and places to hide. In addition, you must learn to crouch and run. While doing so may seem foolish, that very action may save a life. The idea is to make yourself the smallest target possible. Most adults are reluctant to do this because they have not taken such action since they were children, but with practice, this action will no longer feel awkward. This means expending effort a few times each week until your balance and ability are under control. Do not be the person who stands upright, runs in circles, and screams hysterically. If during practice you realize that you are not in shape to crouch and run, it costs nothing to improve this ability with exercise and repetition.

Another essential tactic is to move in a serpentine manner, which essentially means do not run in a straight line, provided that option is available. A zigzag pattern of running makes a person less of a target. Again, multiple decisions have to be made instantly; practice will allow you to do that more easily.

Parking lots and garages

Parking your vehicle close to commercial stores or in a garage near an exit is most likely your best choice. Often, parking lots and parking facilities become assault traps. Make an effort to park in a well-lit area, which makes anonymity difficult for potential assailants, and always use your observation skills when leaving or approaching your vehicle.

When parking within a garage, like the one pictured above, park near other vehicles and as close to an exit as possible. If you cannot park near an exit, make sure you know where the nearest exit is. Approach or leave your vehicle with purpose. When returning to the parking area/facility, place your car key or any key on your keyring between your index finger and middle finger. Should anyone grab you from behind, you can begin jabbing at their eyes, nose, or mouth with the key. It is important to have a high level of awareness while approaching a vehicle. Check under the cars while approaching the vehicle; look for shoes of someone who might be crouched on the far side of the vehicle, awaiting an opportunity to attack. The perpetrator may be there for the purpose of a sexual assault or a robbery. Keep in mind that perpetrators do not like to leave people alive who have witnessed their felonious crimes. Under these kinds of circumstances, again, endurance is important. Probabilities are high that the assailant will want to leave the parking facility and drive the victim to a remote location where the likelihood of being found is reduced significantly. Choosing to go willingly with the assailant will be up to the victim. However, there is at least a chance that the unwilling, combative victim may be saved in a place where others are likely to come along, as opposed to a remote area, where the assailant can totally restrain and kill the person.

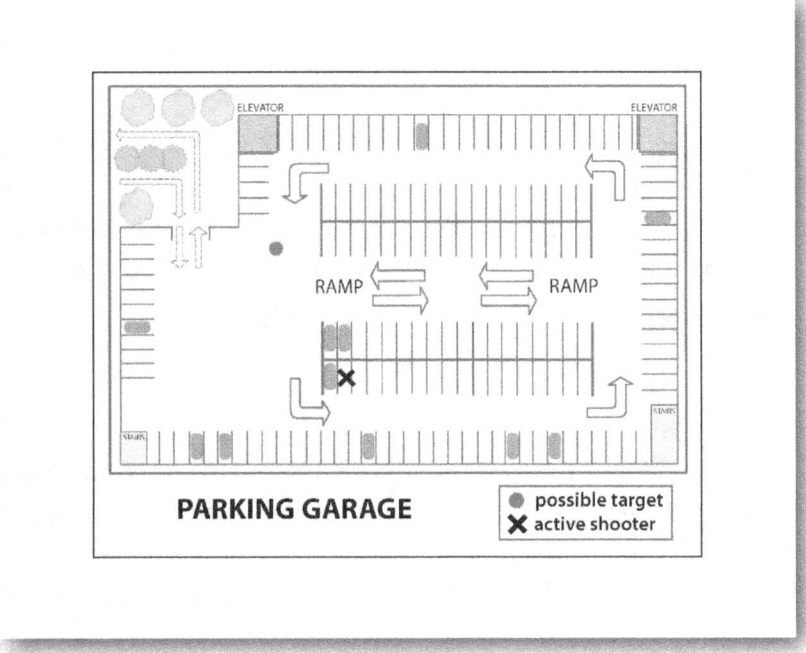

PARKING GARAGE

● possible target
✕ active shooter

If the assailant tries to reassure the victim that he or she just wants money, then there would be no need for the perpetrator to demand that the victim leave the area. If money is all the person wants, then give it to the perpetrator. Otherwise, run and scream as loud as you can. These people do not like it when the event gets out of their control.

When approaching your car, glance backward to catch movement from the corners of your eyes. In addition, while at a distance from the car, you will be able to see the feet of another person standing behind a car, even if the head and torso are not visible. This more than likely means someone is trying to stay out of sight, which could present a danger. While approaching the vehicle, practice looking inside, day or night, to determine whether someone is waiting to attack. If all is clear, use the following sequence of actions to exit the parking area:

1. Get in the vehicle.
2. Lock the door.
3. Start the engine.
4. Put the car in gear.
5. Put the seat belt on.
6. Back out or move forward.
7. Leave as quickly as possible.

When exiting a car, look around and pay attention to the existing scene. Note whether there is someone in a car, walking toward a car, walking toward a building, etc. It is a warning sign when you return to your car and see the same person milling around the parking area who was there earlier. If the scene has not changed since you first left the vehicle, take precautions to ensure your safety.

Recreational facilities

Recreational facilities, such as a lake with beach area, can easily become dangerous. Given crowds of people and rising temperatures, sometimes tempers flare and an otherwise peaceful environment can hold danger. To provide a clearer understanding of a possible situation, Dr. Hill provides this example. It was a sunny summer day, already warm in the morning with stifling heat, while I was on patrol at White Rock Lake, an inner-city park that was heavily used on summer weekends by huge crowds of people. On the day in question, the crowds were composed of a multicultural mixture, and as the temperature grew hotter, there was a growing sense of trouble. A fight broke out between members of a large family who were celebrating an elder's birthday and another family that afternoon. Dr. Hill observed civilized behavior breaking down in phases, until there was an explosion of violent activity. One of the celebrants honoring the elderly woman objected to the use of foul language by the other family. Ultimately, the violence carried over, disrupting yet another family, and within an instant the fight was like a wildfire spreading out of control, from person to person, before the officers could control it.

In response, the city police and parks and recreation staff were able to deploy about twenty-five officers in riot gear, which seemed to further inflame participants. The riotous participants shoved law enforcement aside and continued the quickly growing fight. On that day, I personally observed many injured people who were on the periphery of the fight trying to extricate themselves, only to be drawn into the melee. Violence spread so quickly that by the time adequate forces were called in and deployed, hundreds of people were involved, including dozens of people who had no investment in the fight. Everyone was swallowed up into the fight, leaving the police officers with virtually no effect on the riotous participants. Hundreds of people were involved, and those drawn in created an additional problem—putting the children in harm's way. These children were knocked around, which further infuriated parents and other adults, causing the fighting to become more intense and dangerous. Knives and guns came out. There were gunshot wounds, stab wounds, and wounds from baseball bats, clubs, chains, and other weapons. The lesson to be learned is to not get involved in activities in which there are large crowds of people. In other words, if people are squashed together, agitated, shoulder to shoulder or in such close proximity to cause uncomfortable, defensive feelings, exit the area.

We live in such stress-inducing times that it is rather easy for people to break out of their civilized mode of living and express their anger, disappointment, feelings of being socially strangled (over controlled), and deep resentment spawned by feelings of having been treated unfairly. This emotional agitation is true of perpetrators and victims. It is key to understand how it can impede survival strategies from working.

Some thought should be given to the psychological concept *deindividualization*, which occurs when people feel that they are anonymous while reacting in concert with the will of a large crowd or body of people. As a rule, these people are ordinarily law-abiding citizens, but the group mentality is overwhelming, and they find themselves in a stupor within the group—following along, engaging in the damaging and violent behaviors with other participants. This, of course, is dangerous because they do not care who gets hurt or what they destroy. In interviews after the fight we just described, many people could not believe they had participated and became quite remorseful with guilt feelings, expressing shame. The point of this story is that our own lack of understanding of the dynamics of a situation can create an even greater chance of facing violence.

Shopping malls

We do not expect to encounter violence while shopping in a mall. Unfortunately, such expectations can cause people to become victims of violence.

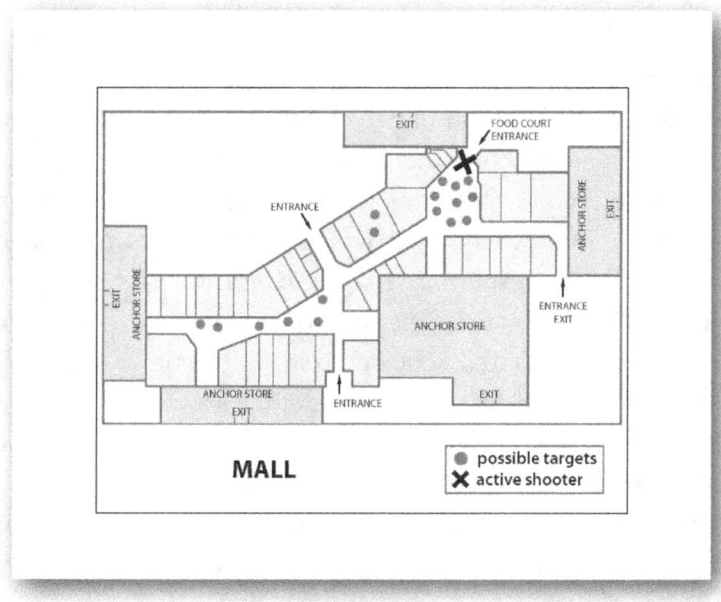

For example, notice the congestion in the food court; the individuals who have congregated here have unknowingly created a target-rich environment and will become caught in the curve. Humans have a hard time shifting from their expectations to the realization that they have just blundered into a violent situation. You have to consider what to do in such a situation, and thereby increase your chances of surviving. Being unprepared for such an encounter will likely cause people to freeze and do nothing at all.

Similar to the other scenarios presented, this environment demands that people use the preventive tactics to complete a recon of the mall, identifying which routes to take to escape, depending on the location of the violence. If no chance of egress is possible, then you should have identified locations within the environment in which to seek concealment/cover. Do not become a victim of the herding effect by joining up with the masses because this becomes a target-rich environment.

Public transit

Public transportation presents a particular problem regarding escape from violence, whether in a bus, on a train, or other forms of mass transit. All passengers are lumped together in a box. It is important to be observant and take note of anyone wearing a long coat or clothing, under which a firearm may be hidden. Likewise, if the conveyance is crowded and you take note of someone pushing others around and moving in your direction, one thing you may assume is that this person may be preparing to attack or kill someone. If it appears that you have no place to hide or means of escape, and when it becomes evident that violence is about to occur, you must decide whether or not to be cornered and killed or rush the attacker. You run the risk of being mortally wounded, but you also may save yourself. One decision you may have to make if the option is available is whether to become a seated passenger or standing one. You must determine whether or not to shield your body with the body of another, or provide a clear target if you rush toward the attacker.

Conclusion

We have listed within each environment the tactics with corresponding actions you can use to support your strategic objectives. We have stated that you can learn these skills, but it does take time, and practice is absolutely required for efficiency. It is now up to you, with instructions in hand, to decide how much time you will devote to practicing the skills on a regular basis until they become second nature. This is another way of asking, how much is your life worth? You may ask, "How do I continue to practice finding cover and concealment or escape and evasion after I have practiced within the environments I am familiar with?" The answer is clear: you must go to unfamiliar places and strategize survival tactics within such unfamiliar locations. Recognize possible exits and places of concealment, and employ listening skills.

Although civilization has brought forth many wondrous creations, ironically it has degraded our ability to be aware of ongoing activities and changing events that may be life-threatening. For example, artistic expression in the media (movies, television, books, etc.), often leave the false impression that we are familiar with the subject matter of violence; however, that knowledge is vicarious. The commitment to stay alive is a commitment to remain aware and vigilant; to renew and use our senses to help our own survival.

CHAPTER 6

Understanding Domestic Violence

This handbook book has addressed the strategies you can use to increase your chances of survival in a violent incident. This chapter takes a moment to visit another potentially dangerous environment—not one where a shooter has a crowd at his mercy, but one where the perpetrator attacks one-on-one in a domestic situation.

Domestic violence has been defined by the journal *Workplaces Respond to Domestic and Sexual Violence: A National Resource Center* as "a pattern of coercive behavior, including acts or threatened acts, that are used by a perpetrator to gain power and control over a current or former spouse, family member, intimate partner, or person with whom the perpetrator shares a child in common."

Although the statistics show that women and children are the primary victims of domestic violence, broader research indicates that men can be victims as well. In fact, we now know that domestic violence affects human beings from all walks of life and does not discriminate according to socioeconomic status, age, gender, race, religion, or education. Furthermore, victims of domestic violence share some characteristics such as low self-esteem, learned helplessness, and a belief in the myths about battering relationships, such as the woman must have somehow "caused" the assault.

In addition, the victims are often traditional, with strong beliefs in the family unit and in the stereotypical feminine role of inferiority and passivity, which allows them to accept responsibility for the batterer's actions. As a result, victims often suffer from guilt but deny the terror and anger they feel. Presenting a passive face to the world, the victims have the strength to manipulate their environment to try to prevent further violence. They believe no one will be able to help them resolve the predicament except themselves. Economically and emotionally dependent on the spouse, they accept violence as normal behavior.

Statistics

According to the Department of Justice (DOJ), Bureau of Justice Statistics (June 2013), 85 percent of women and 15 percent of men were victims of domestic violence. In fact, in the same report, the DOJ estimates that 960,000 domestic violence incidents occur each year; however, only 25 percent of all domestic crimes are reported to the police.

Domestic violence occurs with 50 to 60 percent of all married couples; four to five women are murdered by their husbands or boyfriends each day in the United States. Domestic violence includes physical and/or sexual violence, emotional and psychological tormenting, verbal abuse, financial abuse or control, stalking and/or harassment, and physical intimidation or injury.

According to a 2010 study conducted by the Centers for Disease Control (CDC), released in 2013, "Little is known about the national prevalence of intimate partner violence, sexual violence, and stalking among lesbian, gay, and bisexual women and men in the United States." However, the same 2013 CDC report released the following data concerning the percentages of lesbian, gay, and bisexual individuals who reported experiencing domestic violence:

- 75 percent of bisexual women
- 46 percent of lesbian women
- 47 percent of bisexual men
- 40 percent of gay men

Why a Person Stays

There are many reasons why domestic violence occurs, but this handbook focuses on the reasons most often listed, reasons provided by victims who sought Dr. Hill's help during his thirty-five years of practice as a psychologist.

The reason mentioned most often for not telling anyone about the marital violence is fear. Fear occurs because the victim has already been intimately involved with victimizers in the past and understands what the consequences are for reporting violence. These victimizers include fathers/mothers, husbands/wives, ex-husbands/wives, boy/girlfriends, ex-boy/girlfriends, fiancés or fiancées, work associates, and others. As a rule, these people are male, though women are also capable of tormenting their victims and may ultimately kill them. This category of victimizers instills terror within their victims with the threat of murder. They resort directly to threats to keep their victims under their control. Whatever psychological disorder they may have, these men do not seem to be able to tolerate being in a relationship with a female who will not be controlled. Therefore, they keep their victims on a tight leash. If a victim attempts to break loose, their victimizers become enraged, confront their victims, and begin punitive actions. There are enough incidents reported in the news to make us all aware of what is going on in these relationships.

The second-most-often-mentioned reason for staying in an abusive relationship is shame. The idea of having a few or many people discover the true condition of the relationship is both humiliating and degrading. Women who are victims of domestic violence are certain that others will perceive them to be incompetent and stupid, especially if they initially told their friends and acquaintances how wonderful their partner is. To some degree, the same is true of men who experience domestic violence, with one difference. Some men are reluctant to report domestic violence predominantly because of the stigma attached to being "an abused man." Men who are unable to "control" their partners or complain that they are suffering abuse are perceived as weak by both law enforcement and society. It is important to understand that women can and do initiate domestic-violence incidents; however, the rates at which this occurs may be inaccurate due to underreporting by men. In addition, lesbian, gay, and transgender individuals also experience domestic violence at the hands of their partners, though some would argue that both law enforcement and society largely ignore this phenomenon.

A significant point to recognize is that domestic violence is not about gender or sexual preference, but most definitely about control. The next paragraphs detail characteristics of these batterers.

Batterer Typologies

Batterers, as well as the battered or abused, come from all different demographic groups. In fact, the label of "batterer" and its subsequent description of the behavioral acts of violence until now have sufficed as descriptors. More recent understanding of typologies includes three major groups:

1. *Power and control batterers* use violence mostly in their homes and are primarily motivated by abnormal power and control needs. This group often can choose to stop their abuse with some psycho-education about anger management and sex-role attitude readjustment, although in some cases the psychological manipulation and maltreatment become greater when the physical abuse stops.

2. *Mentally ill batterers* are characterized by a need for abnormal power and control in conjunction with serious psychological problems, including depression, disordered thinking, and obsessive-compulsive behavior, paranoid disorders, borderline traits, and other serious mental illnesses.

3. *Criminal sociopathic batterers* commit other violent and nonviolent crimes, as well as assaults within the home. They are often diagnosed with antisocial personality disorder, for which there is little known treatment at this time. Depending on their degree of psychopathology, incarceration of these subjects may be the only method known to protect battered women or men.

Steps to Leaving

Sometimes society blames the victim of domestic violence with questions such as "Why didn't you leave?" or "Why didn't you go to the police?" Unfortunately, for domestic violence victims, it is not that simple. However, there are steps a person can take to leave a violent relationship:

1. **Leave after the first egregious event.** Do not mistake narcissistic jealousy for love. Do not make excuses for your partner, because this behavior is unacceptable and the violence will escalate.
2. **Make a plan to leave.** If you can leave your partner immediately, then do so and leave all material things behind. However, if the situation and/or the relationship has escalated to a point where you need to exercise caution for your safety, then prepare a strategy to exit the relationship and the residence.
    a. **Pack a bag:** Keep the location of your "go bag" to yourself—store it in your vehicle, at a friend's house, at work, etc.
    b. **Have a place to go.** Let friends, family, coworkers, and anyone else who may be of assistance to you know that you will need a place to stay.
    c. **File a complaint with the police:** Do not minimize the events you report to the police; violence is violence. Believe what you are experiencing because perception is reality, and emphasize that you are scared and in fear for your life.

Special Note

Prior to leaving a violent relationship, victims have additional concerns to address. The October 2013 edition of *Forbes* magazine included several suggestions by divorce financial strategist Jeff Landers to assist those who are ending an abusive relationship. To do so without endangering themselves or other loved ones, Landers recommends taking the following steps:

1. Make copies of financial and legal documents such as bank and credit card statements, documentation of jointly held assets, and tax returns. Keep them in a safe place outside your home.

2. Get a post-office box so that you can receive mail privately.

3. Use a public computer to set up a secret e-mail account to communicate with divorce professionals and other legal professionals. (A controlling or abusive spouse might install spyware on home computers, tablets, or smartphones.)

4. Open a bank account in your own name and start putting money away. If you can, transfer all of your own assets (paycheck, savings, etc.) into a separate bank account.

5. Change all of your PINs to new ones that cannot be identified easily.

6. If possible, remove your name from all joint debt. This protects you from having to pay for anything incurred after you leave.

7. Obtain at least one credit card, and preferably several, in your own name.

8. Acquire a prepaid debit card. These are available at many local retailers, and for a small fee, you can load it up with as much money as you want.

9. If necessary, ask relatives for a loan to hire an attorney and other divorce professionals. This is a time for expedience over pride.

Early Warning Signs

Abusers can be lethal, so pay attention to the warning signs and extricate yourself from that environment as soon as possible. Early action can help you survive domestic abuse and avoid becoming a victim. Critical warning signs that the abuse is escalating include increased frequency and severity of violence; threats to the partner, children, or others; and increased emotional and psychological instability of the abuser, demonstrated through forced or threatened sex acts and/or suicide attempts and threats.

Conclusion

Violence does not occur just in the places where we work or learn, but also in homes across the United States. Domestic violence is an ever-present problem within society and a danger to those who experience it on a day-to-day basis. Unfortunately, it seems only recently that domestic violence has entered societal conversation, which means that it is largely ignored. As a society, we reject violence in public places on unsuspecting victims but accept that violence happens in the homes of our neighbors, colleagues, and acquaintances, as if this type of violence is not as important. We want to emphasize that this type of violence—domestic violence—is real, dangerous, and also unacceptable. However, there are steps one can take to end the violence and an abusive relationship. For those individuals who are not victims of domestic violence but know a friend, colleague, relative, or neighbor who is currently experiencing domestic abuse, you have a responsibility to make a report to the proper authorities to do your part as a member of society, protect members of society, and reduce the possibility of a violent, life-threatening incident.

CHAPTER 7

Being a Captive, Do's and Don'ts

By
Wayne R. Hill, PhD

There is always the possibility of becoming a captive in the midst of a violent incident. Below is a list circumstances in which you may find yourself becoming a victim in a violent incident. These categories are arbitrary but are presented as a means of describing both the type of situation and the category of perpetrator.

Categories of Perpetrators

The Political Extremist or Terrorist

This person rarely operates alone or in an unplanned fashion. He or she is often fanatical and blindly obedient to "superior" orders, apparently willing to make the supreme sacrifice. Impersonal and indifferent to victims, though not necessarily cruel or callous, this person is generally goal-oriented, though that may change as the operation proceeds. The tendency is for these perpetrators to be highly motivated, often subservient to some ideology or cause and eager to maximize publicity. The symbolic meaning of their acts and the need to maintain face are high priorities. They use hostages as shields to ensure escape, such as the seizure of the Israeli athletes at the Munich Olympic Games in 1972 by Palestinian nationalists.

The Fleeing Criminal

This person is frustrated during the course of a crime and, when seeking to escape the scene, takes hostages to try to bargain his or her way out. These perpetrators have learned the technique and witnessed the spectacular success of the political extremist and try to apply those methods to their purposes. The rhetoric of the perpetrator often hides his or her fear. This person wants to deal and maintain dignity at the same time, but is desperately afraid of being cheated and needs "guarantees" of the deal and his or her own safety. Although manipulative, this perpetrator will settle for a great deal less once convinced there is no way out. As an example, consider any one of the numerous bank robbers who try this daily somewhere in the United States.

The Institutionalized Hostage Taker

Because this perpetrator operates in confined familiar surroundings, is desperate, and feels there is nothing to lose, this is one of the most dangerous perpetrators. In addition, this perpetrator is often on drugs or other mind-altering substances. He or she often uses the rhetoric of the political extremist, making wild, unrealizable demands. Harboring deep-seated grievances with a real hatred for authority is the controlling factor in the perpetrator's behavior, resulting in an unwillingness to listen to a rational approach. This person is callous and often deliberately cruel toward victims. His or her level of intelligence is rarely high, but he or she is often street-smart and dangerously cunning. This hostage taker is rarely well-armed but is capable of improvisation sufficient to hold off superior forces. Publicity is often an important feature for this hostage taker. A well-known example occurred in Huntsville, Texas, in June 1974, when Fred Gomez Carrazco, a dangerous lifer and drug "czar," seized hostages in an unsuccessful attempt to escape from the prison.

Estranged Person

Hostage taking can result from family disputes. Intervention by third parties, especially police, can produce a highly charged, irrational atmosphere. The hostage taker seeks to demonstrate that he or she is the master of the situation. Bargaining is impossible while emotions run high, but such people usually want a peaceful end, provided a dignified way out can be found. Often, they will settle for surprisingly little when anger and frustration have abated. Such persons suffer from a temporary mental imbalance but are not necessarily mentally ill. The danger of violence greatly increases when young children are involved. There is often a serious conflict of loyalty among those caught up in these situations. When the hostage taking is a frustrated abduction, the perpetrator may take the view that if he cannot have the victim, no one else will, leading to murder-suicide. Sadly, in many cases, in defiance of a court order giving custody of a young child to the mother, the father takes matters into his own hands.

Person Laboring under a Sense of Grievance or Injustice

This person has a "public" sense of having been wronged. He or she has often tried, unsuccessfully, to resolve matters and sees hostage taking as a chance to publicize grievances and put matters right. Many of these people see themselves as representatives of a particular group. They cannot be argued out of their beliefs, however irrational, and any attempt to push them is likely to produce a violent reaction. The hostage taking is often carefully planned and executed, but with little thought to the resolution. Such hostage takings are often a disguised "cry for help," but the indifference of the hostage taker to the victim is not calculated to generate sympathy. Publicity has a high priority for this perpetrator, who wants moral rather than material satisfaction.

For example, consider the workplace shooting and hostage crisis perpetuated by former ESL Inc., employee Richard Farley on February 16, 1988. Farley worked as a software engineer for ESL, a company that worked on government contracts. Unfortunately, Farley spent four years stalking a fellow employee, Laura Black, after she rejected his romantic advances. Finally, Black filed an order of protection against Farley in January 1988, resulting in the termination of his employment with ESL. Angered by the inability to see Laura Black and convinced that his coworkers had commiserated with Laura against him, Farley packed the trunk of his car with firearms and drove to the ESL building on the afternoon of February 16, 1988. Farley later claimed to law-enforcement officials that all he wanted was to confront Black and urge her to rescind the order of protection against him; if she refused, Farley had planned to commit suicide. However, Farley did not try to speak with Laura at all; rather, he entered the ESL building shooting at any person within his visual purview. Farley shot and wounded four former coworkers, including Laura Black, and killed seven. He barricaded himself in the ESL building; the remaining employees hid as best they could in offices and under furniture while the police attempted to communicate with Farley and save the hostages. After several hours, the police negotiator was able to convince Farley to surrender for a turkey sandwich and a soda.

Religious Fanatic

This person is closely related to the former category and to political extremists. Unworldly, often irrational attitudes are colored by extreme prejudice and bigotry. Total conviction of the righteousness of the perpetrator's cause is often coupled with a morbid sense of persecution. Actions often are characterized by a high degree of cruelty toward victims, who are seen as infidel representatives of the group against which the struggle is directed. The hostage taking itself often has deeply symbolic overtones and is veiled with a mystical or religious quality.

Religious fanatics are so wrapped up in their beliefs that they seem insensitive or oblivious to the feelings of others. They are particularly resentful of challenge by similar, but unallied, religious groups. The "cult-ist" element must never be overlooked. On December 15, 2014, an Iranian immigrant living in Sydney, Australia, held hostage dozens of patrons of the Lindt Chocolate Café in downtown Sydney. Man Haron Monis was a fifty-year-old, self-proclaimed Sunni Muslim cleric and spiritual healer. Monis was an independent religious fanatic acting of his own volition and was well known to law-enforcement authorities, having been previously charged as an accessory in the murder of his wife. He also was charged with forty counts of sexual assault during his time as a spiritual healer. However, on Monday morning, December 15, 2014, Monis was only interested in perpetuating his fanatical religious ideology when he held seventeen peo-ple hostage inside the Lindt Café. He forced some of the hostages to place their hands on the café window, while others held up a black flag, adorned with the *shahada* or the Muslim Testimony of Faith: "There is no God but God, and Mohammed is the prophet of God." Monis made demands of law enforcement using the hostages. Some hostages contacted the media via phone; others posted videos to YouTube documenting their plight. After five of the hostages managed to escape, Monis became enraged and could be seen through the café window ordering the hostages around. Law en-forcement negotiated with Monis for sixteen hours; however, when talks between Monis and the negotiator finally broke down, Australian police raided the café and shot Monis. Sadly, two hostages also were shot during the course of the raid.

Mentally Disturbed Person

This is perhaps the most dangerous category because behavior is unpredictable. Often capable of functioning extremely well and with considerable cunning, many of these perpetrators suffer from severe illnesses, of which paranoia is a dominant symptom. Hostages are taken in defense of what these perpetrators perceive to be in their interests. Such a distorted and volatile scheme of rea-soning often requires skilled professional assistance to detect, understand, and unravel. Such persons are out of touch with reality and will not respond to logic.

There is great explosive potential in such situations because the perpetrator is invariably insensitive to the victim as a fellow human being. Great care must be exercised to avoid antagonizing the perpetrator by word or gesture. Many have suicidal and homicidal tendencies to which hostage taking may be simply a prelude. Consider Dylann Roof, a young, white male who shot and killed nine African Americans inside the Emanuel African Episcopal Methodist Church in South Carolina. Investigative work showed that Roof had planned the massacre months in advance; he believed his actions would increase racial tension within the United States, leading to a race war, as well as punish African American individuals for wrongs that Roof perceived had been committed against white people. Roof went to the historic black church on June 17, 2015, and joined an ongoing prayer group. The twelve church members unwittingly became Roof's captives when they invited him inside the church and welcomed him to their prayer group. He was never going to let them leave alive.

Roof sat with the group for approximately one hour, listening to their conversations and prayers, waiting for the perfect moment to begin shooting at the victims. Interestingly, Roof admitted to authorities that he almost changed his mind about committing the massacre because the church members were so kind to him, but in the end, it did not matter. Roof eventually stood up, looked at the prayer group, and said, "I'm here to shoot black people." Even as one church member tried to reason with him, begging him to spare their lives and let them go, Roof shot them anyway, stating, "No, you've raped our women, and now you're taking over our country." Sadly, the prayer group discovered that the connection they believed they had made with Roof would not save them. This is in keeping with earlier advice that you cannot count on prior relationships to save you during the commission of a violent act.

Becoming a Hostage

As a former Dallas police officer, I have been involved in numerous calls for service that involved a perpetrator trying to avoid being arrested by means of barricading himself while holding a victim as a human shield.

First, it is very common for the police to answer a call about a domestic disturbance including violence. At the scene, usually a man and woman are fighting about a domestic issue. When the police arrive and interrupt the couple, the male often panics, barricading himself in a bedroom or bathroom, threatening the police by saying, "Don't come in; I will kill her." Now the victim becomes the perpetrator's human shield. Of course, it is not necessary for the perpetrator to actually go into a room and shut or lock the door. The human shield is a barricade in and of itself.

Second, this may occur by accident when a person unknowingly stumbles onto a crime while it is unfolding. Typically, the innocent victim does not at first realize what is happening but soon discovers he or she is a captive. Most likely the perpetrator panicked and impulsively grabbed the closest victim. Following this action, the perpetrator will realize that he or she is trapped and is now also guilty of kidnapping. Panic will increase, and that is a dangerous moment because the perpetrator will not likely know what to do (i.e. how to extricate him or herself from the incident).

It is very important that such victims keep their wits about them by not becoming simultaneously panicked with the perpetrator. One can anticipate a dismal outcome under those conditions because a shooting could easily take place or other violence be perpetrated against the victim. During this time, listening skills become a premium. Those skills should be put to use in a silent attempt to determine what is wrong with the perpetrator and his or her state of mind. Do not ever try to verbally address the perpetrator's problems. Such attempts may throw the perpetrator into a rage, reminding this person that others are always try to exert control over him or her.

Use the following analogy to help you understand the mind of such a perpetrator. Imagine standing far away from a two-story building. Obviously, the easiest floor of the building to see from a long distance away is the second floor. In this analogy, the perpetrator's psychological problems can best be seen at a distance because they are above the surface. It is preferable for victims to recognize the problems above the surface. You want to survive the encounter.

To go forward with the analogy, as one gets "closer to the building" (the longer you are held by the perpetrator), the first floor is more easily observed. You will find the shallow underpinnings of the perpetrator's problems on the first floor; his or her issues may become more transparent. Your captor may be throwing up emotional flack all over the place. Remember to act interested but not curious. Take it all in, and remember to make small gestures, such as a slight chin nod, to prove that you are listening. If you have been actively listening, it will not be as hard for you to deduce what's going on beneath the surface. Try to be silent about your deductions. Most people hate to be diagnosed. It makes them feel transparent, as though you can read their minds. As a response, perpetrators often become very paranoid or if not paranoid, very suspicious, distrustful, and often agitated.

Keep in mind that in the bowels of the building it will be murky, a basement filled with extensive pain that is constantly stirred up by a raging wild thing trapped in physic unconsciousness. According to the model, no matter how skilled you may be, it is a disastrous idea to take even one step down the stairway into the basement because it contains psychological material that your captor has kept under wraps all of his life. Even an attempt to go down there will be met with great resistance and likely end with your death.

The victim, the perpetrator's human shield, may hear some very depressing words from the perpetrator. At such times, many perpetrators begin talking about their current crisis and how it matches up with the life they have led. The victim may hear the perpetrator make remarks such as "Nothing ever works out for me, and they are going to kill me because I have kidnapped you." As a victim, you must be careful about making comments because they may not be welcomed, such as selling the perpetrator on the idea that things are not as bad as he or she thinks. It is important to listen carefully to the story. If the captor requires a response, indicate that you are listening. Or say, "I hear you." If your captor demands your judgment concerning what he or she is saying, try sticking with a comment such as "If I understand you correctly," and then follow up with the summary of what he or she has said to you. Do not try glossing everything over, and avoid confronting the reality with him or her. If the captor asks you a question, try to be as neutral as possible; certainly you do not want to offer judgment. This will become a difficult balancing act because there are some recommendations you should become aware of:

- Do not panic; keep your wits about you.
- Don't stare at the perpetrator, but do not look away unless you are told to do so.
- He or she may require you to look at him and if he does, you should comply. However, do not stare fixedly into his eyes. Doing so may remind him of someone who did that when they punished him as a child. The outcome may be disastrous because the captor may form a negative transference fixation to you.
- Be interested in your captor. Do not give him or her shallow solutions to the present complicated dilemma.
- Do not be condescending; he or she will know immediately that you are insincere and will punish you. Your captor may take great pleasure in making you pay for sins committed by someone else. And one other thing—hearing your cries for the pain he or she is inflicting is proof positive that the cries of pain are not his or hers.
- Do not try to talk the captor out of his or her feelings because he or she may have decided long ago not to trust anyone. Whether you agree or not with what the person is saying, nod slightly as though you are taking it all in. Study your captor, keep your assessment to yourself, and try to deduce what he or she is planning.
- If he or she asks what you think, say you are listening and trying to understand.
- Do not try to fake him or her out.
- Do not tell the person that you understand what he or she is going through.
- Do not promise him or her that everything will be all right.
- If the person asks you to speak to the authorities for him or her, reply that you will do so. Do not go into great detail about what you would say to the authorities unless you are asked to explain.

- You might tell your captor that it sounds like others have not understood him or her or have been unfair.
- You may tell him or her that you do not believe he or she intended to hurt anyone.
- Keep your comments short and precise.
- Do not make comments such as, "After all, you have not killed anyone." For all you know, he or she may have killed a carload of people.
- Keep your own remarks to a minimum. It is the captor's show, and he or she is the major player.

We have been saying for years that people are dying to have someone listen to them and then killing because no one will.

Because this handbook is designed to help you develop strategies to survive a violent incident, it might be beneficial, if you are interested, to engage in role-playing activities to understand how to respond as described above. Finding a partner who is willing to act through a hostage scenario might be helpful in developing the dialogue skills described in this chapter.

Debriefing

When the hostage event is over and you have been rescued, I can promise that you will be debriefed. Do not become angry about being debriefed. The police do not know you and cannot know whether you were a willing participant from the beginning or if you were just unlucky. They will want to confirm your identity and check criminal records to see if you have been involved in any criminal activities.

Second, there very well may be a mental health professional on the scene to help the police determine if you are suffering from post-traumatic stress disorder. Among other things, the mental health professional will certainly examine you for the *Stockholm syndrome*. Some of the symptoms include a positive feeling by the prisoner toward his or her captor and negative feelings toward his or her own family and friends, as well as authorities. Perhaps the most well-known case took place on February 4, 1974, when Patricia Hearst was kidnapped at age nineteen. Patty was the daughter of media mogul William Randolph Hearst. The reason for the kidnapping by the Symbionese Liberation Army (SLA) was an attempt to gain a large ransom from Patti's father. The FBI arrested Patti in September of 1975 on bank robbery charges, and sentenced her to thirty-five years in prison. However, President Carter pardoned her after he was convinced that she suffered from the Stockholm syndrome. As mentioned, the hostage has positive feelings about his or her captor and also supports the captor's reasons and behaviors for felonious actions. This is also referred to as *traumatic bonding* due to a powerful and eminent fear of loss of life. It has been noted that after a person has been rescued from a hostage situation in which Stockholm syndrome results, the captive or victim often supports the thoughts, beliefs, and demands of the captor. Captives have been known to make embarrassing and humiliating statements to the press, causing difficulties in their future endeavors.

Conclusion

There is always a chance in a violent incident that you will be taken as a hostage. Perpetrators may either accidently or purposefully decide to take hostages. Understanding the captor's state of mind and the particular factors that might motivate him or her offers you some insight into how to protect yourself in such a situation. Also, reviewing the typical scenario of what occurs in hostage taking and understanding appropriate responses as a hostage are more steps in arming yourself with useful strategies and skills for surviving the incident. Keeping calm, using active listening, and maintaining vigilance about everything that is going on around you are key steps in managing a hostage situation.

CHAPTER 8

Treatment of Post-Traumatic Stress Disorder Victims

by
Wayne R. Hill, PhD

Much time has passed since I began a career as a mental health professional in 1974. During the last four years of my police career, I served as staff psychologist for the Dallas Police Department's Psychological Services. Post-traumatic stress disorder (PTSD) was just gaining recognition as a legitimate mental illness, and we began treating officers for PTSD. My approach to the treatment of PTSD victims was shaped to a large extent by police street experiences. I became quite familiar with some of the emotional problems that were directly related to PTSD. Most importantly, this disorder was likely to be found among officers and others who had been involved in, or were in close proximity to, a high-risk event, such as a brush with death.

From those early years to date, I have encountered a number of people who have suffered with PTSD after experiencing a traumatic event. These untreated men and women were still in emotional pain several years after the event. Of the people who were in treatment, their initial complaints were about the effects of free-floating anxiety and clinical depression. These elements I am about to discuss would likely cause a victim to feel afraid. Their fears became cyclical; the compounding of fear caused their fear to grow. This led to an anxiety neurosis that was difficult to break. Some of the hallmark features of free-floating anxiety include changes in body temperature, from hot to cold and clammy, as a victim's body engaged in physiological changes in an effort to stabilize body temperature. Because human beings rely on making sense out of nonsense, these sufferers incorrectly concluded that they must be having a heart attack. This then often led to adopting well-known symptoms of a heart attack:

- Irregular, pounding heart rate
- Difficulty breathing
- Pressure in the chest
- Dry mouth
- High-pitched ringing in the ears
- A sharp, piercing pain shooting down the left arm

Terrified and grasping for answers, victims had no problem rushing to see the doctor about a heart attack. But when the examination and test results were negative, revealing no physiological difficulty, doctors often found resistance from their patients to the suggestion that their problems may be psychological. These people were so desperate to make sense out of what is happening to them that many would rather have had a heart attack than admit to psychological problems.

A number of patients were afraid that they were going crazy. Interestingly, when the heart-attack scare was put to rest, many victims—perhaps most of those with free-floating anxiety—next looked toward cancer, usually of the brain. Finally, after the terror caused by anxiety became *so* terrible that it became overwhelming, patients would seek psychological help.

Upon first entering psychotherapy, most of these women and men had no clue about the depth and seriousness of their emotional condition. Many were living destructive lives. Others had become alcoholics, feeling empty and without purpose, living hollow lives. Those with untreated PTSD still remained unhappy people with little prospect for change. Some victims divorced their life mates. Or conversely, the traumatized victim was left behind, largely due to poor communication, resulting in a shallow understanding of the anger, depression, and anxiety that often caused them to withdraw from others, such as people at work, their neighbors, and family members.

Although most of them were trying to understand what went wrong with their lives, rarely did they connect their difficulties with having experienced a traumatic incident. As time passed, I came to understand that people from all backgrounds are subject to the effects of a traumatic incident. In those earliest years, I thought that one must be directly involved in a PTSD incident to be traumatized. That is not true. A person may observe a traumatic event unfolding, in which he or she was not involved directly but remained on the periphery as a witness to the event. Furthermore, being on the scene while the event is ongoing is not required if the event is serious enough to evoke symptoms of PTSD. I refer to this population of victims as the forgotten victims of PTSD.

It is sad to know that many people are living difficult lives due to a disorder that is misunderstood but very treatable. The road to recovery begins with an education about PTSD early warning signs. Officers who have been traumatized as the result of having chosen perhaps one of the most difficult occupations and making important sacrifices for their communities have paid an unfair and often unbelievable price for the privilege of serving their fellow citizens. But what about those people who are victims of PTSD and are not members of the police community? They, too, suffer from the same symptoms as others.

PTSD Defined

As a rule, post-traumatic stress disorder was primarily defined, rather haphazardly, by a composition of symptoms rather than any definite statement regarding how people become traumatized and or what to do about it. Interestingly, one of the most important diagnostic features of PTSD, according to treatment professionals in the early years, was whether or not the person was experiencing flashbacks. In other words, if a patient did not have flashbacks, then there was no trauma. That was problematic because not every traumatized victim experiences a flashback. In fact, the most prevalent symptom has always been free-floating anxiety. This means that periodically the victim is totally overwhelmed with an anxiety attack, and since the victim receives no relief from his or her anxiety, the episodes gradually worsen until they became full-fledged panic attacks.

C. Scrignar, author of *Post-Traumatic Stress Disorder: Diagnosis, Treatment, and Legal Issues*, 13 (2nd ed. 1988), was one of the first psychiatrists to describe PTSD as being an enduring mental illness. Here is how he describes it:

> Any environmental stimulus which poses a realistic threat to life or limb, impacting on one of the senses, or more likely a combination of the five sensory pathways to the brain, if perceived as a serious threat to one's life or physical integrity (whether it produces injury or not) can be regarded as a trauma and precipitate a PTSD. It is not necessarily the type or duration of the environmental trauma, but whether the trauma poses a perceived realistic threat to life or limb and that the person is consciously aware and has a full appreciation of the potential for serious injury or death to self or others. Also vital and a natural consequence is an intense activation of one's autonomic nervous system following exposure to the traumatic event. (13–14)

After the first few years of treating victims of PTSD, mental health professionals agreed on a unified definition that was incorporated into the *Diagnostic and Statistical Manual of Psychiatric* Disorders (DSM). Listed below are five criteria listed for individuals with symptoms, according to the *DSM*, to assist in the diagnosis of PTSD.

Criterion A: A person has been exposed to a traumatic event in which both of the following were present:

1. The person experienced, witnessed, or was confronted with an event or events that involved actual or threatened death or serious injury, or a threat to the physical integrity of self or others.
2. The person's response involved intense fear, helplessness, or horror.

It is important to reinforce the fact that elements one and two of **Criterion A** must be present. Keep in mind that sometimes these factors are delayed due to defense mechanisms that prevent a victim's real feelings from surfacing from the unconscious to consciousness.

Criterion B: The traumatic event is persistently re-experienced in at least one of the following ways:

1. Recurrent and intrusive distressing recollections of the event, including images, thoughts, or perceptions. As stated before, intrusive thoughts can manifest at any time and are often confused with the flashback symptom. These reoccurring intrusive thoughts bore their way into consciousness, stimulated by some unconscious factor within the victim's environment. It could be a sound or color or anything else that reconnects the victim to the traumatic event. Victims often spend a great deal of emotional energy attempting to suppress the recurrent intrusive thoughts, which is just the opposite of what needs to be done. Such invasiveness is torturous to a victim who wishes nothing more than to be at peace.

2. Recurrent distressing dreams of the event.

In my opinion, although a dream associated with the aftermath of a traumatic event is disturbing, dreams do not have to be about the specific traumatic event with regard to PTSD. Typically they are not biographical as a matter of fact. Most of the time, dreams following a PTSD event are night terrors that disrupt sleep, over and over. This cycle leaves the victim tired, lethargic, and unable to cope.

3. Acting or feeling as if the traumatic event were recurring; this includes a sense of reliving the experience, illusions, hallucinations, and dissociative flashback episodes, including those that occur on awakening or when intoxicated. In this case, victims may have literally had a psychotic breakdown.

4. Intense psychological distress at exposure to internal or external cues that symbolize or resemble an aspect of the traumatic event.

5. Physiological reactivity on exposure to internal or external cues that symbolize or resemble an aspect of the traumatic event. Victims may be seriously affected by seeing someone who reminds them of the traumatic event. Common examples include robbery, confronting a burglar in one's home, unanticipated death of a loved one, infidelity, and many other issues. Severity can be determined by using **Criterion A.**

Criterion C: Persistent avoidance of stimuli associated with the trauma and numbing of general responsiveness, not present before the trauma, as indicated by three or more of the following:

1. Efforts to avoid thoughts or feelings associated with the trauma

2. Efforts to avoid that arousal or cause a recollection of the trauma

3. Inability to recall an important aspect of the trauma (*psychogenic amnesia*)

4. Markedly diminished interest or participation in significant activities

5. A feeling of detachment or estrangement from others

6. Restricted range of affect, (e.g., unable to have loving feelings)

7. Sense of a foreshortened future, (e.g., does not expect to have a career, marriage, children, or a normal life span)

The first four factors listed below are indicative of clinical depression, and the last three are associated with *dissociative reaction*. Although not mentioned before, dissociative reaction includes an out-of-body experience. Typically, victims will feel like they are outside of themselves, watching themselves as opposed to feeling that they are inside themselves. This can take the form of standing next to oneself or float-ing above oneself, watching from above. It is a defense mechanism that puts some distance between the PTSD event and one's feelings about the event.

Criterion D: Persistent symptoms of increased arousal, not present before the trauma, as indicated by two or more of the following:

1. Difficulty falling or staying asleep
2. Irritability or outbursts of anger
3. Difficulty concentrating
4. Hypervigilance—feeling a need to be on guard at all times
5. An exaggerated startle response

Criterion E: Duration of the disturbance where symptoms in **Criteria B, C, and D** last or more than one month.

Criterion F: The disturbance causes clinically significant distress or impairment in social, occupational, or other important areas of functioning.

PTSD Symptoms

We often hear of people who have experienced PTSD, whether from cata-strophic circumstances or from very questionable claims. It is important to note that the severity of a case can range from mild to very severe due to a delayed effect. However, there are examples of questionable validity, like the incident in which a woman who, while shopping in a grocery store, slipped and fell on a wet floor. Subsequently, she filed a lawsuit alleging that the fall caused PTSD. She alleged that she had been traumatized by the fall and the aftereffects of pain and humiliation.

Another incident involved a man who had the unpleasant experience of watching a "made for television movie" that had been advertised as being about child sexual abuse. Even though he alleged that he had been sexually abused as a child, and a warning had been given to viewers prior to the start of the movie, he chose to view it anyway. According to his story, later that night he awoke from sleep with the feeling that he had been psychologically traumatized. Unfortunately, trauma can be a money maker for unethical people. However, even though insincere people can create a glitch, hundreds of others benefit from treatment every day.

As stated before, PTSD is on the rise as a popular diagnosis. As a result, one problem is that the popularization of PTSD potentially reduces credibility for those who legitimately suffer from it. Historically, it has been difficult for police personnel at all levels to accept PTSD as a legitimate disorder. The same kind of skepticism is often found among mental health treatment professionals. Lack of acceptance of this disorder stems from an educational deficit and misunderstanding about the disorder. Police officers are in just the right profession to experience the kinds of events that are particularly traumatizing. For the general population, excluding police and war veterans, events occur every day that can be traumatizing.

Over the past thirty years, I have treated a large number of police officers who were traumatized in the line of duty. Traumatic incidents are common place on the "police beat." During most officers' careers, they should expect to experience their share of execrable incidents. Often such events are so emotionally painful that they cannot cope with the feelings that are engendered, resulting in PTSD.

In most cases, they were confused about their condition. I believe that although most police officers are familiar with some of the most commonly associated, or classic, symptoms of PTSD, such as flashbacks, this disorder often causes a great deal of confusion. For example, a person may be confused with general stress response or the emotional after of an upsetting episode of one kind or another.

Probably the most erroneous belief is that those who are affected by PTSD are in some way inherently weak or defective. Conversely, a person might easily fail to recognize the onset of acute or chronic depression and/or anxiety as being symptoms often associated with PTSD syndrome. There seems to be a lack of understanding about trauma generally, but even less is understood about the connection between a traumatic event and associated repressed material from an earlier time in the victim's life.

Perhaps many children and others manage to repress earlier traumatic events effectively. If so, those feelings may have been sublimated. (Sublimation occurs as a process when noxious events must be relegated to the unconscious mind by means of defense mechanisms that were in the service of the consciousness.) However, if feelings from an early life trauma join with the feelings of a late life trauma, the victim gets double-dipped. Confusion is the chief product because the feelings from two different events must be processed.

Therefore, education about PTSD and the treatment of it is essential.

Treatment of PTSD

Although there are many approaches to treating PTSD, I believe certain aspects of treatment are not readily understood. Some specific treatment aspects, in particular those relative to psychodynamic factors, are most often not well understood. The information that follows represents my own professional view and understanding of the treatment of patients who are stricken with PTSD.

Years of treating numerous PTSD victims have convinced me that while treatment professionals should be open to ideas from various treatment modalities, some of the most difficult patients respond best, over the long haul, to psychodynamic theory and treatment. This being said, it is also true that Cognitive Crisis Intervention principles, in the beginning of treatment, are essential for more immediate, decompressive results. It allows victims time to tell their stories and access a therapeutic condition in which they are encouraged to think back over an incident and to fill in the blanks in their story. It produces an environmental condition that encourages trust. Therapists must provide stability. Victims must be allowed to work at a basic level in psychotherapy until a therapist can assess whether or not it is time to move on.

Choosing a Mental Health Professional

There are many mental health professionals to choose from for therapy. Here are some suggestions for selecting a professional who can serve your needs:

- Choose a licensed professional: counselor, social worker, or clinical psychologist.
- Choose someone who seems interested in you.
- Choose a professional who is smart.
- Choose a professional who has experience with PTSD.
- Ask the treatment professional what kind of cases he or she has worked on and if the treatments were successful.
- Remember that the treatment professional works for you and is sworn to help you and in no way hinder your recovery.
- If you feel unsure, ask your family doctor whom he or she would recommend;
- There are no shortcuts to getting positive results from psychotherapy therapy; stay away from people who think this process takes only two or three weeks.

Conclusion

This chapter discussed the ill effects that violent incidents can cause—specifically PTSD—as the most problematic results of being in a traumatic event for anyone, law-enforcement officer or victim. Remember, in the aftermath of a violent incident, a person may feel psychologically unbalanced. The likely outcome of not seeking professional guidance, if identifying with any of the PTSD symptoms, could lead to further emotional instability.

I do not believe that a person can live through a horrendous event without being traumatized. A person must express the energy attached to a PTSD event to relieve the strain of trying to keep feelings locked up inside. Therefore, it is important to seek help from professionals who have been trained to help a person recognize and adjust to the symptoms of a traumatic event.

CHAPTER 9

Conclusion and Recap

No one wants to be caught the in the middle of a violent incident. Yet, based on the escalating number of violent incidents, it is likely that you will witness or experience at least one significantly violent incident in your lifetime. Violence is an unfortunate part of our lives, and it cannot be ignored or wished away. Despite the horrors associated with a violent event, it is possible to affect, to some degree, how individuals respond to a violent incident, thus improving their potential for survival.

To achieve a significant positive effect, you must adopt a new and radical way of thinking. The process begins by asking yourself some critical questions, such as "Are you committed to staying alive?" and "Do you have the right to live?" Another important question is existential: "Would you take a life to save your own life?" In addition to changing your thinking, you also must adopt the following skills:

1. **Proactive skills:** You must choose to be proactive and thereby increase the odds of survival. While you are not required to become a self-defense expert, you must practice the simple but powerful skills that have been outlined in this handbook. They must become second nature so that you continue to upgrade your ability, while you grow more confident in their use. We want you to think of this handbook as a tool that provides alternatives to acting impulsively or taking no action at all.

2. **Ingrained responses:** Remember that people who are unfamiliar with violence typically react to violence in one of three ways: fight, flee, or freeze. Those who have not taken the time to find ways to extricate themselves from a dangerous situation will most likely freeze, which can result in disastrous consequences. Taking the necessary time to understand what to do will increase your chances of survival.

3. **Active observation:** We have emphasized conscious and purposeful surveillance of your surroundings at all times and encouraged you to make strategic choices that give you the best chances for survival. For example, when going out to dinner, choose a table in a restaurant where there is a clear view of the front door and exits. When approaching your parked vehicle, be cautious by remembering the instructions about safely returning to your vehicle. With regard to parking, remember to continually survey the whole parking area, but avoid staring at your car; this is part of active observation. You must train yourself to sense violence through active observation and raising your consciousness.

Through active observation, you will learn to notice behavioral details about people with whom you share the same environment from moment to moment. Take notice when a person looks out of place or when a person's facial expression does not match his or her posture; this is cause for further observation. This kind of skill is accomplished by becoming more acutely aware. Active observation enables you to remain vigilant or to dismiss your concerns. Awareness of others around you is tantamount to gathering intelligence by observing a person's actions, clothing, or statements, all of which are potential warning flags.

Your understanding of verbal statements can be enhanced by using the table in chapter 4, titled "*Verbal Indicators of Violence.*" Potentially, these indicators can tell you when a person has made a statement or remark that seems aggressive, threatening, inappropriate, or just nonsense. Your observations may lead to nothing, but that does not mean that your skills lead to inaccurate information. Remember to keep quiet about what you are learning so you will not be labeled as being over reactive.

You have a responsibility to prepare yourself to survive a violent event. And when you have vital information, supported by strong evidence, you then have an obligation to inform authorities.

4. **Crisis intervention:** Many people believe that the police are the cavalry and are coming immediately to save them from danger. With all the high-profile violent incidents, you now know that idea is a myth. It can take several minutes for help to arrive after emergency personnel have been notified of a violent situation. The police will eventually come, but it is up to you to advocate for your safety and remain alive until the police can assist you. Learn to regard yourself as the first line of defense and as the primary crisis manager when violence occurs.

5. **Gathering intelligence:** We discussed the need to gather intelligence for your own benefit. We emphasized good listening skills and pointed out that you should practice remaining on the periphery of a crowd instead of getting in the middle. This is particularly true if someone is on their soap box whipping up a crowd. Their rhetoric might deteriorate into angry and aggressive language that is filled with delusional content. When that happens, leave immediately.

6. **Murderers:** We discussed some classification of murderers and hypothesized about their motives. Ultimately, we concluded that the trait they hold in common is that they have killed people. Remember, you cannot count on a previously positive relationship with a murderer, and you should not delude yourself into believing that such a relationship will save you. While most people may believe that murder is indicative of psychosis, this is not true. The most common reason for murder is passion. The second most common reason is power and control of another.

7. **The fact that perception is reality:** Human beings seem to have been born with the need to make sense out of nonsense. However, all things being equal, you should trust your perception. If you believe you are in a dangerous situation, most likely you are. Extricating yourself from that position should be your primary concern. Don't dismiss your perception by going into a state of denial and falsely believing *This can't be happening to me.*

8. **The curve**: Review the diagram on the topic of getting behind the curve. In this case, we are referring to a literal curve that takes into account the sweep of a firearm discharging right to left, left to right, driving victims into a funnel formation that becomes a target-rich environment for a shooter.

9. **Post-traumatic stress disorder**: Most people will need treatment for PTSD following their involvement in a violent and traumatic incident. Recognize that typically the anxiety will be free-floating, which means it has no obvious source; be alert for and avoid any stimuli associated with trauma, difficulty sleeping and concentrating, and/or angry outbursts. Seek help from a licensed professional who has had experience in the treatment of PTSD.

We hope this handbook has empowered you to become responsible for your safety by becoming skilled in the use of survival tools. By becoming more intuitive about your surroundings, whether in a park, parking lot, theater, or other public places, you will heighten your awareness of the intentions of other people through their actions or statements. As we stated in the introduction, you must be able to help yourself survive a violent incident.

Acknowledgements

We would like to thank the following people:

Annie Hill, wife and mother who spent so many hours encouraging us and also reading and editing drafts of this work.

Tony Olivas, loving husband and son-in-law, who lent his expertise as a Senior Federal Air Marshal with the United States Federal Air Marshal Service (retired) and former Lieutenant for the Federal Bureau of Prisons to this work; he reminded us that there was an audience for our handbook.

Terri Reisig, a professional educator, who inspired numerous individuals to become writers, and she also became our very wise editor and friend.

Amy Weldner, a friend, teaching colleague, and talented artist who consulted on the cover for our handbook.

Ghislain Viau of Creative Publishing Book Design, who created the cover for our handbook.

Paula Mintek, of InMyHead Designs, a family friend and artist who spent so many hours creating various drafts of the diagrams used in our work.

Appendix A

Below is a chart listing characteristics of various types of killers. Please note the similarities.

Some Characteristics of Murderer

Stranger-to-Stranger	Serial Killer	Mass Murderer	Spree Killer
Murders accidentally.	Is organized, very specifically planned vs. disorganized, a spontaneous type.	Is a misfit.	Seeks revenge.
Nothing is personal.	Murders victims one at a time.	Feels misunderstood.	Desires admiration.
Victim is in wrong place at wrong time.	Selects victims carefully, or opportunity presents itself.	Is disenfranchised.	Seeks public recognition for acts.
Victim is chosen at random.	Suffers a buildup of tension.	Has injustice detectors (paranoid personality disorder).	Plans poorly for escape.
Victim is killed for resisting	Fueled by fantasy.	Endured many emotional insults.	Lacks empathy.

Stranger-to-Stranger	Serial Killer	Mass Murderer	Spree Killer
Is eliminated as a witness.	Has an expanding fantasy.	Feels devalued.	Attacks victims in a target-rich environment.
May panic following the crime.	Perfects the fantasy.	Feels powerless.	Celebrates his or her violent acts.
	Sees victims as pawns.	Feels disconnected.	
	Has no empathy, remorse, or regret.	Will have made a coded warning statement.	
	Feels no human connection.	Feels driven to murder.	
		Is in a dissociative state.	
		Feels society is too corrupt to save.	
		Does not care who is killed.	
		Thinks everyone deserves it.	
		Is committed, no turning back.	
		During act, has no empathy, regret, or remorse.	
		Killing others empowers him/her.	
		Event plays out in one location.	
		Is committed to dying.	

GLOSSARY

Active observation—Requires a person to become as conscious as possible of all things happening around him or herself while deselecting or filtering issues by level of importance at the moment.

Cognitive dissonance theory—The theory that we act to reduce the discomfort (dissonance) we feel when two of our thoughts (cognitions) are inconsistent.

Cover—To hide from view using an object or other protective impenetrable structure.

Concealment—To hide from view while remaining susceptible to harm from projectiles.

Deindividuation—The loss of self-awareness and self-restraint occurring in group situations that foster arousal and anonymity.

Dissociative reaction—An altered state of consciousness in which a person may engage in behavior like sleepwalking, or experience a dreamlike state, amnesia, or fugue.

Denial barrier—Denial is a defense mechanism employed by the superego structure so a person can resist the feeling of failing to be perfect. Denial also helps block out circumstances that could be dangerous or psychologically damaging.

Drive reduction/tension reduction—The idea that a physiological need creates an aroused tension state (a drive) that motivates an organism to satisfy the need.

Focused listening skills—Listening purposefully to what others say; listening to the tone of voice used to determine the meaning behind what is said.

Herding effect—Using the actions of others as a guide to sensible behavior rather than acting independently.

Information drive—A drive that humans use to gather information about their environment.

Injustice detector—Individuals who present with characteristics of paranoid personality disorder tend to interpret the actions of others as intentionally threatening or demeaning; they believe that people are malicious and that those they encounter are looking to exploit or betray them. Over a period of time, people who possess these characteristics begin to resent others and may act out against them.

Intelligence gathering—Acquiring important information that can be used to assist an individual in decision making.

Prairie-dog peeking—To gather visual intelligence quickly from a place of concealment, while remembering to change the height of viewing from one peek position to another, without establishing a pattern.

Proactive—Acting in anticipation of future problems, needs, or changes.

Stockholm syndrome—A psychological condition wherein a captive begins to sympathize or identify with his or her hostage taker(s).

Unconscious—According to Sigmund Freud, a reservoir of mostly unacceptable thoughts, wishes, feelings, and memories.

BIBLIOGRAPHY

Beasley, J. (2004). Serial murder in America: Case studies of seven offenders. *Behavioral Sciences and the Law*, 22: 395–414.

Diagnostic and statistical manual of mental disorders: DSM-5. (5th ed.). (2013). Washington, D.C.: American Psychiatric Association.

De Becker, G. (1997). *The gift of fear: Survival signs that protect us from violence.* New York, NY: Dell.

Fallon, J. (2013). *The psychopath inside.* New York, NY: Penguin Group.

Felson, R., & Massoglia, M. (2011). When is violence planned? *Journal of Interpersonal Violence*, 27:753.

Festinger, L. (1957). *A theory of cognitive dissonance.* Stanford University Press, Stanford.

Fox, J., & Savage, J. (2009). Mass murder goes to college: An examination of changes on college campuses following Virginia Tech. *American Behavioral Scientist*, 52(10), 1465.

Freud, S. (1950). *The interpretation of dreams.* (AA Brill) New York, NY: Random House. (Original work published in 1900.)

Gidez, C. (Producer). (2013). *Dark knight.* ["Dates from Hell," Season 2]. New York, NY::Sharp Entertainment.

Kalish, R., & Kimmel, M. (2010). Suicide by mass murder: Masculinity, aggrieved entitlement, and rampage school shootings. *Health Sociology Review*,19(4), 451.

Kraemer, G., Lord, W., & Heilbrun, K. (2004). Comparing single and serial homicide offenses. *Behavioral Sciences and the Law*, 22:325–343.

Langman, P. (2012, Spring). School shootings: The warning signs. *Forensic Digest.*

Landers, J. (2013). This domestic violence awareness month, begin to secure your financial future. *Forbes Magazine Online*. Retrieved from www.forbes.com/sites/jefflanders.

Meyers, D. (2014) *Psychology.* (10th ed.). New York, NY: Worth Publishers.

Saddock, B., Saddock, V., & Ruiz, P. (Ed.). (2009). *Kaplan and Saddock's comprehensive textbook of psychiatry.* Philadelphia, PA: Lippincott, Williams, & Wilkins.

Scrignar, C.B. (1996). *Post-traumatic stress disorder: Diagnosis, treatment, and legal issues.* New Orleans, LA: Bruno Press.

United States Department of Justice, Bureau of Justice Statistics. (2013). *Domestic violence/ abuse statistics.* Retrieved from http://www.statisticbrain.com/domestic-violence- abuse.

Waters, M., Chen, J., & Breidling, M. (2013). *The national intimate partner and sexual violence survey (NISVS): 2010 findings on victimization by sexual orientation.* Retrieved from www.cdc.gov/violenceprevention/pdf/nisvs.

Workplaces respond to domestic & sexual violence: A national resource center. (n.d.). *The facts on the workplace and domestic violence.* Retrieved from www.workplace.org.

Zimbardo, P. (2008). *The Lucifer effect: Understanding how good people turn evil.* New York, NY: Random House.

About the Authors

D r. Wayne Hill resides in Traverse City, Michigan. He is a licensed psychologist in Michigan and former president of Management and Behavior Consultants, P.C. Now retired, Dr. Hill was appointed psychologist emeritus by his colleagues and partners. He is also a former police officer, having served in Dallas, Texas. His law-enforcement experience coupled with his career as a psychologist allowed him to provide consulting and training services to police agencies nationally. He maintained a private practice and was staff psychologist to the police department in Traverse City, Michigan, as well as staff training psychologist to the Pennsylvania State Police Department's Employee Assistance Program.

Aimee Olivas resides in Bristow, Virginia. She has a master's degree in forensic psychology and specializes in threat assessment. She worked for the Federal Bureau of Investigation (FBI) as an analyst and outreach specialist. Mrs. Olivas is currently a psychology instructor at both the secondary and postsecondary levels. She teaches Advanced Placement Psychology at a Northern Virginia high school and introductory psychology courses at Northern Virginia Community College, where she is an adjunct professor.